BOWLING

HOW TO PLAY, COACH AND WIN

BOWLING

HOW TO PLAY, COACH AND WIN

**Mark Davis
and Sam Collins**

Published in the UK in 2012 by
John Wisden & Co.
An imprint of Bloomsbury Publishing Plc
50 Bedford Square, London WC1B 3DP
www.wisden.com
www.bloomsbury.com

ISBN 978 1 4081 4655 2

Rules on dangerous and unfair bowling (page 60) and modes of dismissal
(pages 125–6) reproduced by permission of the England and Wales Cricket Board.

A CIP catalogue record for this book is available from the British Library.

Designed by Greg Stevenson
Cover photograph © Getty Images
Photographs on pages xi, 23, 25, 31, 35 38, 41, 43, 49, 52, 58, 61, 70, 73, 88, 90, 92,
99, 104, 105 and 114 © Getty Images
All other photographs © Grant Pritchard
Illustrations by Greg Stevenson

This book is produced using paper that is made from wood grown in managed,
sustainable forests. It is natural, renewable and recyclable. The logging and
manufacturing processes conform to the environmental regulations of the country
of origin.

Typeset in 11 point Joanna by Saxon Graphics Ltd, Derby
Printed and bound in Great Britain by Clays Ltd, St Ives plc

CONTENTS

FOREWORD

Bowling hurts. It really does. Even spinners hurt (but they won't get any sympathy from me). The 'quicks' get the real pain. I don't know why we do it. Why would you run in all day and bowl as quick as you can on a block of, what is virtually, concrete? There's got to be a little of the sadist, and the stupid, in most bowlers, especially the ones that try to bowl fast.

I try to bowl fast. I've never been the fastest around, not by any stretch, but I've always tried. I hit the pitch, I ask questions. If it swings, brilliant, if it doesn't I hope for some 'nibble' off the wicket. But most of all I want bounce; some consistent carry to the keeper. I may try for it but I don't care too much for sideways movement. I don't care too much for a green seamer either. I just want some bounce, and I'm pretty sure that's what most bowlers want. If I'm going to run in and bang that ball in 120 times a day I want my bouncer to get up. I want my good length balls to carry to the slips. I want my bad balls to be hit away. I want a good, fair cricket wicket.

But that's not always what we get. And that's part of bowling; the ability to change tactics and draw upon different skills if conditions don't favour you. Work out your 'stock' ball; this is the ball that you go to for the majority of your overs, spells, games and career. The one you can bowl without thinking about it. It'll be a part of you, and it will define you as a bowler. On top of that comes the energy you bring, the fight, the aggression, the guts and determination to do a job that is going to hurt you at some stage.

There is no way around it, it's a matter of 'when' not 'if' you are going to be injured. We do what we can to try to avoid injuries, but they happen. I've always hated the gym but I have it to thank for staying 'reasonably' injury free in my career. Weights for strength and power, the mats for core work and stretching, the treadmills and bikes for cardio sessions; I hated them all, but they were the necessary evil.

Why do we put ourselves through it? That feeling of bowling a beauty, completing a maiden, sticking to a plan and eventually picking up that well-earned wicket. I don't mind the gift wickets either, the bad balls that get nicked or chipped up, I'll take them all, but the ones that are hard earned, toiled for, are the real prize.

I've had great battles with some of the best batters in the world, some all-time greats. I love those days. I've had successes, I've had failures too, and plenty

of them. It's all part of the battle, bat vs ball; me vs them. Days to savour and days to forget; well, not to forget, but to learn from. But the biggest battle was with myself. I forced myself to blog about what went on in my world when I was playing, to reflect on each day's play and my own performance. I know it made me a better player. I made myself work out why I had a good day or why I had a bad day; why my rhythm was great or why my 'demons' dominated me. I enjoyed the psychology of the sport, working on blocking those 'demons' (the anxieties, the negative self-talk, the self-doubt) and replacing them with a clear(ish) mind. It doesn't always work, some days they are too strong, but without it there is no way I'd have the success I have had.

It hurts, gym work is boring, the long hours in the field on low slow wickets, the mind games, the time away from home, the sweat, the blood, the sore feet, the blisters, the injuries (toes, ankles, knees, hips, back, shoulders, elbows, fingers...), the rehab, the bouncer laws, the into-the-wind end, not getting a bat (or only a very short one) in the nets, being expected to win or not lose a game with the bat, getting fully padded up and not batting, left-handed batsmen, your batsmen not scoring enough runs, net bowling, dropped catches, very hot and humid places, wrecking multiple pairs of expensive bowling boots, runs to third man, hotels, shorter careers than batsmen, the media (sometimes), ice baths, balls that don't swing, small boundaries and last-wicket partnerships.

Welcome to bowling. I don't know why we do it.

Actually I do. We love it.

Iain O'Brien
(WELLINGTON, LEICESTERSHIRE, MIDDLESEX AND NEW ZEALAND),
SEPTEMBER 2011

INTRODUCTION

Bowling is the most important thing in the game. It's the brainiest part of cricket.
H.M. HERMAN, WRITER, 1937

The quick bowlers can come out from behind the sofa now, Iain's gone.

There are so many different types of bowler, such different personalities involved that it seems strange to categorise them as the same species. Yet they all live on planet cricket, and while they're there they face the same conditions and the same natural disasters (the Virender Sehwag typhoon perhaps), and all have to adapt to survive.

That adaptation can take on different forms – new deliveries, new tactics, different fields. Most levels of cricket are played across three platforms now – declaration, 40–50 overs and Twenty20 – and a bowler needs to be resourceful if he is to succeed across all three.

But let's strip it back for a minute. Being a bowler is a privileged position. When the bowler gets that ball in their hand, they know they have total influence over that next delivery. If they can put enough pace, swing or spin on it they know that no batsman in the world will be able to get near it. When the ball actually does hit those stumps it's a great feeling.

Pace bowlers, off-spinners, leg-spinners, swing bowlers, doosras, Chinamen – there are plenty of ways to hit those stumps or take wickets. If you need further proof, take a look at Sri Lanka's Lasith Malinga, a man with an action so extraordinary he could be skimming stones.

There will always be a place for the unorthodox alongside the orthodox bowler. It's where the ball goes that matters. Listen to coaches, read coaching books, but along the way the bowler should try to develop a technique that works for them and stick to it. This book is there to help the bowler understand their action, and why the ball behaves as it does when they do different things to it.

Read it, learn it, apply it, and then read it again.

THE BASICS

1.

There's more in bowling than just turning your arm over. There's such a thing as observation.
WILFRED RHODES, YORKSHIRE AND ENGLAND SPINNER

TERMINOLOGY

'Line and length' are terms fundamental to any bowler. Generally bowling a good line and length refers to bowling the ball in an area where it is riskiest for the batsman to play an attacking shot. The line is off-stump, and the length sees the ball pitch between two to three metres in front of the batsman. The orthodox response to a ball landing in this area would be a forward defensive shot.

Being able to bowl a consistent line and length is actually the bowling equivalent of a forward defensive – the backbone of any bowler's game. Without the control this gives, any bowler will struggle to contain the batsman. The more occasions the bowler can repeat a good line and length, the more successful he will become. (The pitch maps of the great bowlers would show very close groupings of length and line – the lesser the bowler, the more erratic the distribution.) A good line and length will differ for a spinner, but if ever a seamer is in doubt, he can always retreat to the suggestion that the best line and length to aim for is to pitch the ball so it will go on to hit **the top of off-stump**.

Once a bowler has mastered bowling a basic line and length they can move onto other variations, such as swing, or spin, or learn tricks like the slower ball.

Not every ball bowled in cricket is of a perfect line and length. On the following pages are explanations that might help the bowler to understand further the subtleties that different lines and lengths bring with them.

Line

Line refers to the direction in which the bowler bowls the ball. For example, a ball heading in the direction of off-stump would be said to have an off-stump line, a ball on leg-stump, a leg-stump line and so on.

Depending on whether the bowler is a swing or seam bowler, the ideal line to bowl is generally to probe on or just outside the off-stump. This puts doubt in the batsman's mind as to whether they should commit to playing a shot or leave the ball alone, whichever way the bowler may be trying to move the ball, and this uncertainty can lead to mistakes in judgement and possible dismissal.

A tight line (offering no width) will restrict the batsman's ability to free their arms, limiting their stroke play and run-scoring options. This in turn will create and build pressure on the batsman, giving added chance that they will lose their composure.

Bowlers might look to change their line for a particular batsman. A bowler looking to get a batsman out bowled or LBW might bowl a straighter line, but with that comes an increased risk of being hit for runs through the leg-side. Similarly, an out-swing bowler might look to bowl outside of the off-stump to tempt the batsman into driving away from their body in search of an edge.

Tactical bowling can also be tailored around field placements. A captain might ask the bowler to bowl a specific line in an attempt to restrict the batsmen's scoring option. An example would be to pack the off-side with fielders and bowl consistently a foot outside the off-stump.

Below is a suggested list of ideal lines to the right-handed batsman for different types of bowlers:

- **Out-swing** bowler – middle and off, swinging away.
- **In-swing** bowler – two stumps outside off-stump swinging in.
- **Seam** bowler – on or just outside off-stump.
- **Off-spinner or Chinaman** bowler – three or four inches outside off-stump, spinning it in towards the wickets.
- **Left-arm orthodox or leg-spinner** – middle-and-off spinning towards the off-side.

Remember – A bowler can control the line they bowl the ball by making sure that their action comes through in a straight line at their target. This process is made easier by a controlled, straight approach to the crease, and a straight follow-through, although these are not imperative.

The best length is the shortest you can bowl and still get the batsman playing forward.
DOUGLAS VERITY REPEATING THE WORDS OF HIS FATHER, ENGLISH SLOW LEFT-ARMER HEDLEY VERITY

Length

Length refers to the area on the pitch where the bowler pitches the ball, which in turn is decided by when they let go of the ball.

The ideal length is one which, when pitching, the batsmen is unsure whether to play forwards or back. This is known as a good length. Generally, a good length for a spinner will be fuller than that for a quick bowler.

Pitching the ball on the perfect length means the ball will swing, seam or spin (depending on the bowler) in a way that gives the batsmen very little or no time to react positively to the movement.

What constitutes a good length can depend on the type of surface a bowler is bowling on. A general rule is that a good length delivery will go on and hit the top of the stumps after pitching. If the playing surface is firm the bowler will bowl shorter to hit the right length and, conversely, if the pitch is soft then a fuller delivery is required.

Once the bowler can bowl their stock length on demand, variation of length can also be important to keep the batsman guessing. An example of this would be bowling a few short of length deliveries with the occasional bouncer to get the batsman's weight set up on their back foot, leaving the batsman potentially susceptible to the good length delivery.

LINE AND LENGTH

Full toss: 2 metres from the crease

Half volley: 2–4 metres

Good length/back of length: 4–8 metres dependent on type of surface, bowler and batsman

Bouncer: 8 metres or more

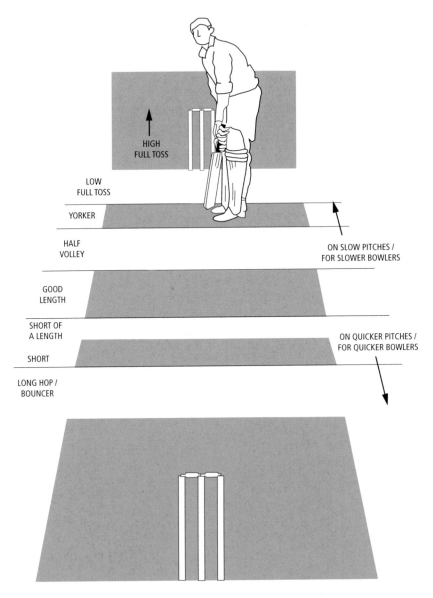

OTHER TERMS

Long hop

What it is: The long hop is the ball batsmen love and bowlers dread. It's a short ball lacking the pace to trouble the batsman, and most likely will cost the bowler four runs.

Where does it pitch? Closer to the bowler's feet than the batsman's.

Bouncer

What it is: The quick bowler's long hop, but because of the extra pace it is an excellent aggressive weapon for the fast bowler. A good bouncer should target the batsman's armpit rising to the heart, or get up at their throat. If the bowler is bowling to a compulsive hooker, they should try to get the ball above head height of the batsman, so that they lose control of the shot. Discussed in more detail on page 59.

Where does it pitch? Halfway down the wicket, or just inside the bowler's half depending on the surface.

Short of a length

What it is: Confusingly this can be either a good ball or a poor ball depending on the surface. If it's wide it'll most likely be thumped, but if it's straight it can rush the batsman on a quick pitch.

Where does it pitch? Fuller than a bouncer, shorter than a good length.

Good length

What it is: A good length is that length which leaves the batsman uncertain of whether to play forward or back. Normally this is about four metres from the batsman although, if the surface is slow, the ball should be pitched fuller.

Where does it pitch? On the length where the batsman is unsure whether to play back or forward.

Half-volley

What it is: Probably four runs. The half-volley lands in the perfect slot for the batsman to hit the ball just as it bounces, so negating any seam or swing the bowler has put on it. It's sometimes worth throwing in the odd wide half-volley, because batsmen can become careless when they are driving with their arms away from their body.

Where does it pitch? On the perfect length for the batsman to reach it as it bounces.

Yorker

What it is: A lethal delivery if the bowler can bowl it to order, the yorker can knock a batsman off his feet and knock his stumps over. Called the 'toe crusher' as it pitches on the batsman's toes, it is a delivery with real wicket-taking potential when bowled with pace and swing, and is particularly effective against new batsmen, tail-enders and in one-day cricket, where it is very hard to score off. Discussed in more detail on page 63.

Where does it pitch? On the batsman's toes.

Full toss

What it is: The only problem with the yorker is that when the bowler doesn't get it, it is a full toss. And this is essentially a free-hit for the batsman, to be avoided if possible.

Where does it pitch? It doesn't.

Beamer

What it is: One step worse than the full toss, a beamer is a ball that reaches the batsman on the full above waist height for a quick bowler, or above shoulder height for a slow bowler. An extremely dangerous delivery to a batsman who is expecting the ball to pitch, this is a delivery to be avoided at all costs. A beamer will be called a no ball by the umpire, who can remove the bowler from the attack at his discretion.

Where does it pitch? On the batsman.

BASIC BOWLING

INTRODUCTION

Those are the principles of bowling, now it's time to learn how to bowl the ball. To do that, the bowler will need to know how to grip the ball, what a bowling action actually is, and eventually how to add a run up to it.

If the bowler is ever experiencing problems in the future, they should look again at the basic technical details that they will learn in this chapter. Bowling is simple if it is allowed to be.

The grip

What it is

Pick up a cricket ball. Look at the seam and run your fingers over it. Throw the ball from one hand to the other for a few minutes, playing around with putting your fingers in different places around the seam to see if you can get it to spin in different ways using your wrists and fingers.

That's gripping a cricket ball in its most basic form. When it comes to bowling the ball, the bowler has to be a bit more deliberate about their grip, as how they choose to grip the ball determines what they are trying to get the ball to do and how successful they will be in doing so. Different types of swing, seam and spin all have different grips that will be explained over the pages of this book.

How to do it

 The seam is vertical. The bowler's first two fingers are placed on either side of the ball; their thumb is placed underneath the ball resting on the seam.

The grip of the ball should be loose enough so that the ball can be taken out of the hand with little difficulty. There should be a small gap between the back of the ball and the hand. The wrist must stay upright and behind the ball; the pressure points of the ball should be close to the tips of the fingers.

Practice drills

 The bowler should use a half-red, half-white coloured ball and practise throwing to a partner no more than 10 paces away, keeping their wrist behind the ball like a bowling action. The seam should stay upright and the red and white colours should appear constant. If not, slightly adjust the position of the fingers on the seam. They should practise flicking their wrist as they release.

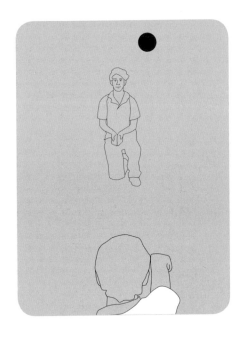

The bowling action

What it is

When the bowler has got used to gripping the cricket ball it's time to move on to how they actually go about bowling it. The release of a cricket ball is called the **bowling action.** The bowling action refers in its various parts to the **run-up**, the **jump and pre-delivery**, the **delivery** and the **follow-through**, all of which will be explained in more detail in this chapter.

Whatever type of ball the player is looking to bowl – quick or spin – the basic principles of the action are the same. It's only how they dress it up afterwards, with different grips and speeds, that determines what type of bowler they are.

Different types of action

Confusingly there are three main types of bowling action. Each has different advantages, it is important that the bowler does what suits them best. They'll only really discover which applies to them when they start working on the run-up and delivery stride.

It used to be thought that a **side-on** action was the bowler's best chance of extracting maximum pace and movement away from the right-hander. However, the rise of several significant bowlers with **front-on** actions, not least Malcolm Marshall and Wasim Akram who both moved the ball prodigiously at great pace, has proved this theory inaccurate. While it is true that different actions favour different types of swing movement, a strong wrist position can be enough to counteract any difficulties.

For any young bowler when learning their bowling action, first check how their feet land in the delivery stride. This is the natural position from which they can then align their hips and shoulders. If their hips/shoulders/feet are not aligned then a **mixed action** will result. If the mixed action is not corrected there is potential for the bowler to suffer serious injury to their back, due to unnatural twisting of the spine at the point of delivery.

EXPERT COACHING TIP

Always get a qualified coach to check that your action is safe and not mixed.

Side-on

What it is

The traditional style of bowling, the side-on action is used by those bowlers who want to get the ball to swing away from the right-hander.

DENNIS LILLEE (Australia 1971–84)
Lillee had a textbook side-on action that allowed him to curve the ball away from the right-handed batsman.

How to do it

 The back foot lands parallel to the crease at 90 degrees.

Front foot points towards leg-stump.

Hips and shoulders are in a side-on position in line with the back foot.

Look outside the front arm.

Front-on
What it is

A delivery style that involves less twisting of the back, this style helps the bowler to swing the ball in to the right-handed batsman.

MALCOLM MARSHALL (West Indies 1978–91)
The late Malcolm Marshall was a famous front-on bowler, proving that bowlers could trouble batsmen with in-swing and generate great pace from the front-on action.

How to do it

 Back and front foot must point down the wicket.

 Hips and shoulders in line front-on.

 Looking inside the front arm.

Why do different actions help balls to swing different ways?

Swinging the ball is all about a strong wrist-position, and keeping the wrist behind the ball for as long as possible.

With a side-on action the wrist naturally tails towards the slips, as the action takes the front arm down past the left pocket, favouring the out-swing bowler.

With a **front-on** action the wrist shapes towards fine leg, and the front arm comes down towards the back pocket, helping the in-swing bowler.

Coupled with the right grip, the shine of the ball on the right side, and the right style of release (out-swing – slide the hand towards fine leg; in-swing – push wrist through towards first slip), this gives the best chance of swing. Swing is explained in more detail on page 42.

Mid-way

What it is

Neither one nor the other – a compromise action that allows the bowler to swing the ball either way. It's important to check that the alignment does not slip into a mixed action or injury will occur as the bowler's spine is being forced to twist unnaturally at the point of delivery.

BRETT LEE (Australia 1999–2008)
Lee grew up with a genuine mixed action, with the bottom half of his body predominantly side-on, and the top half front-on. To avoid injuries, he adjusted his arm position from across his chest to more front-on giving him a mid-way action, allowing him to generate pace and swing without putting so much strain on his back.

How to do it

- Hips and shoulders in line, feet point at a 45 degree angle.

- Eyes looking through front arm and directed towards target.

- Before bowling off a full run-up, it is important to practise and master each section of the bowling action. The following will refer to a right-arm, side-on bowler.

Stationary bowling
How to do it

- Stand at right angles to the intended line of delivery. The back foot is parallel to the crease.

Lift the non-bowling arm up vertically, with a slightly bent elbow and looking behind the front arm. Place the bowling hand under or close to the chin. Lift the left knee up.

With the front arm, the bowler should imagine they are pulling a chain; this will drive their head towards the target. The bowling arm scribes a big circle often referred to as the figure six.

Release the ball from the highest position possible, the head and eyes must stay level. Allow the back leg to pick up, drive through and let the arms go through to complete the action.

EXPERT COACHING TIP

Statics are useful for the beginner, but as you develop, a walk or jump into the action can be beneficial as it replicates your normal bowling action.

Throwing

Throwing is one of the great debates in cricket. It is illegal for the bowler to throw the ball, a term easily defined by the straightening of the bowling arm while delivering a ball.

If the square-leg umpire deems the bowler's action to be a throw, they will be no-balled, and possibly stopped from bowling again in the match. With luck, if there is anything suspicious about a bowler's action their coach will have already spotted it. If a bowler does have a suspect action, it is most likely to be visible clearly in their effort ball (like a bouncer or a quicker ball).

Much of the debate in the professional game concerns bowlers with unusual joints that enable them to do extraordinary things with the ball, for example Shoaib Akhtar and Muttiah Muralitharan. There have also been concerns about straightening of the arm during the delivery of the doosra, the off-spinner's variation ball.

As it stands, bowlers are allowed to straighten their elbows to a maximum of 15 degrees as they deliver the ball.

The jump and pre-delivery

We'll deal with the run-up in more detail a little later, but this links the run-up to the delivery – it is where the bowler takes off during the run-up prior to delivering the ball. As the bowler jumps into the air, it allows the turning of the body with the left shoulder and hip to be pointing towards the target; this is called the side-on action (see different types of action, page 11). In preparation for the delivery stride, the bowler will then position their body to release the ball.

Key points for the jump and pre-delivery

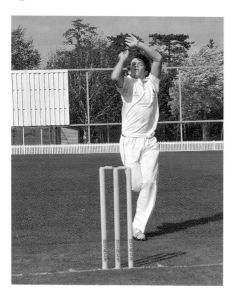 Take off from the left foot.

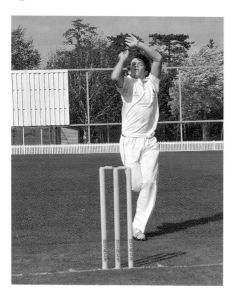

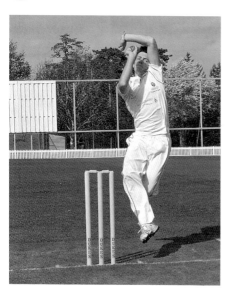 Turn 90 degrees in mid air (for the side-on action).

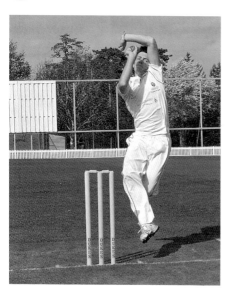

Land with the right foot parallel to the crease and then move into the delivery stride.

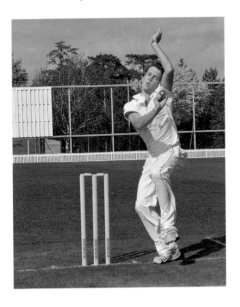 

Weight should be evenly balanced.

Back foot lands side-on or parallel to the crease.

Front arm (non-bowling arm) is raised and pulled back.

Front knee is raised in line with front elbow.

Head and eyes stay still and level.

Bowling hand under the chin.

Keep body weight on the back leg.

The delivery stride

The delivery stride is the actual point of releasing the ball.

Key points for the delivery stride

Back foot side-on, parallel to the crease. Front foot points to fine leg.

Eyes level, focussed at the target. Keep the front leg braced, and try to release the ball from the highest possible point.

Front arm (non-bowling arm) pulls down towards the target. This generates the power to enable the bowling arm to come through and the back leg to drive through close to the front leg.

The follow-through

The follow-through is the completion of the action as the bowler moves on down the wicket.

Key points for the follow-through

🏏 The bowling arm completes the full circle and goes past the left pocket.

🏏 Head and eyes still level, and focussed at the target.

🏏 The body still drives straight for the target as the bowler's momentum carries him to a natural conclusion some way down the wicket.

Caution: follow-throughs can be dangerous!

Bowlers can't just run down the wicket as they please in their follow-through. The spikes on their shoes can cause the wicket to rough up, making life difficult for the batsman, and potentially providing unfair advantage for spinners. Because of this, regulations are in place that state the bowler must never run through onto the business area of the pitch. The bowler should get used to running off the wicket in the follow-through when bowling in the nets.

Practice drills

- Place collapsible cones in a line at the take-off point. The bowler jogs in from a few paces and practises jumping over the cones, taking off on their left foot, turning 90 degrees in preparation for the movement into the delivery stride. Move on to using six-inch training hurdles. Repeat the process but increase the tempo. The bowler should throw their arms into the air to gain more height.

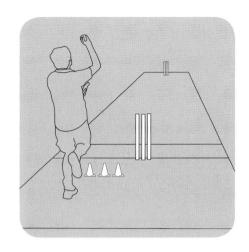

- Once mastered, move on to using a cricket ball and begin bowling at targets.

- If in a sports hall, use a line across the hall and try to land the ball on a line. If on grass, use a long piece of string as the intended line to bowl. Remember to keep head and eyes level and drive towards the target area.

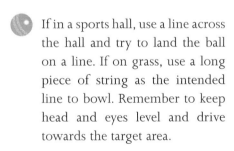

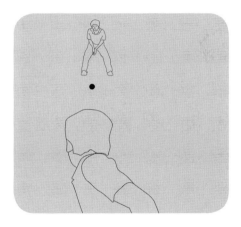

- Place a set of cones in an area of good line and length. See how many times the bowler can hit the target area. The more successful the bowler becomes, reduce the size of the target area.

- Work in straight lines. Check at each stage of the bound, delivery stride and follow-through that the feet are working on the same line.

The key is to drill the left, right, left combination. Take off with your weight on your left foot (your right foot goes in the air as does your right arm). Turn in mid air, land with your right foot and then your left comes down ready for delivery. It sounds tricky but it isn't.

The run-up

The whole point of a run-up is to put you in the best possible position at delivery to bowl the type of ball you want to bowl.

Approaching the crease

If you spend enough time watching, listening to or reading about cricket it won't be long before someone talks about Michael Holding's run-up. You'll probably hear the words 'mesmeric', 'effortless', 'languid' accompanying it too, and with good reason – Holding's approach to the wicket was a mobile lullaby that saw him nicknamed 'Whispering Death'. The 'death' came because it preceded an action capable of delivering a cricket ball with a brutality few have equalled before or since. So don't neglect the run-up. It's worth getting right, because it gets the bowler to where they need to be to bowl the ball.

Away from Holding for a second, the run-up should be like an aeroplane taking off; a smooth and balanced approach moving up through the gears as the bowler gets closer to the stumps and delivery. Different bowlers start their run-ups in different ways – shuffling, walking, running – the only constant is that the stride pattern as the bowler approaches the crease should be like their natural running style – remember rhythm.

The whole point of the run-up is to get the bowler in the best possible position for delivery, so the pace with which they reach the crease should be the best for them to get into position to perform their bowling action. Be careful – too slow and they will have no momentum, too quick and they will be unable to control their action. They must keep their head and eyes still and focus on where they are going to pitch the ball.

The bowler shouldn't be suckered into thinking that if they want to bowl quick they have to tear into the wicket from miles away either. A run-up should suit the action. If a bowler gets their pace from shoulder rotation or a quick arm then they might not need such a long run-up, while there's no point in them haring in from 30 paces if they are going to be exhausted after two overs. Those bowlers who do rely on a sprinter's approach are a dramatic sight – Waqar Younis, Brett Lee, Shoaib Akhtar – but these approaches would have been developed over a long period of time and accompanied by specific fitness routines.

There have also been plenty of quick bowlers who bowled off shortened run-ups. Wasim Akram operated off 15 metres, while the former England bowler Simon Jones found he could bowl the same pace off a five-yard or 20-yard run-up, but preferred the 20-yard run as it put less strain on his body at the crease. It may also be that the bowler might choose to operate off different length run-ups depending on the type of pitch they are playing on. Dennis Lillee developed a shorter run-up for use on pitches that he knew would not be so suitable for out-and-out quick bowling.

The ideal angle for the run-up has been a contentious issue in recent times. Young bowlers have been encouraged to look to bowl in straight lines – a straight approach and a straight action supposedly minimising stress and waywardness. Yet a slight angle in the run-up can be a help to the side-on bowler. Two of the most accurate and successful bowlers of recent times, indeed ever – Glenn McGrath and Shaun Pollock – even incorporated a slight step into the stumps in their angled approaches. This meant they were bowling as close to the stumps as possible

Michael Holding approaches the wicket.

– a wicket-to-wicket line that cramped the batsman for room and accentuated any movement of the ball off the seam and in the air.

Three words to sum up the run-up:
*   Consistent   •   Smooth   •   Rhythmical

Spinner's run-up

A quick bowler looking at a spinner might think he has it easy. A couple of paces, a twirl of the arm and that's it – none of this pounding in over-after-over. While it's true, a spinner's run-up is generally shorter, it's just as important for their delivery stride. In fact, a spinner's run-up is vital in how much turn they'll get from their action, as the slightest imbalance at the point of delivery might throw the whole thing off kilter. Essentially then, the spinner's run-up relies on the same principle as the fast bowler's – consistency, smoothness and rhythm in approach.

There's no set pace that a spinner should approach the wicket – just look at Shane Warne and Anil Kumble, two vastly successful leg-spinners over the last two decades yet two totally different approaches. Warne's approach to the wicket was little more than a slow walk, relying on shoulder rotation for his big turn, while Kumble bounced to the crease like a hyperactive rabbit and used the extra pace to help his skiddy style. The bowler should do what suits them, and what feels natural, while giving them a good delivery position. At the same time, if a bowler wants to be the next Warne, it's worth remembering that the immense power in Warne's shoulders made his walk to the wicket something of a freak.

The other thing for a spinner to consider in their run-up is their front foot. The spinner must take care not to deliver the ball until after they have planted their front foot. The front foot acts as a pivot for the spinner's body, allowing them to put maximum turn on the delivery. If the spinner's arm is coming over before the front foot has been planted, it will dramatically reduce the amount he spins the ball.

So each spinner should take some time working out which run-up suits them, and gives them the position and angle for delivery that makes best use of their spin and flight.

Anil Kumble (left) and Shane Warne (right). Two legspinners, but two very different approaches.

How do I get a run-up?

Firstly, the bowler should decide whether they want to start their run-up from a static position or by walking on to a bowling mark. Either way, they must push off or hit the bowling mark with the same foot on each occasion. The next step is to stand (or walk on) at the batting crease line. The bowler then runs away from the stumps into the outfield. When it feels right, they should go through their bowling action, marking the spot, then repeating the process several times to check that they are landing on the same spot and are happy with the run-up. Now they can run in and bowl normally.

When the bowler is happy with the run-up they can measure the distance with a tape measure. Every time the bowler practises or plays in a match, they should measure out their run-up. An alternative way would be for the bowler to cut a length of string the distance of the run-up and keep it in their bag. Many professionals mark their run-ups at both ends of the ground with white aerosol prior to the match. Some bowlers prefer to mark their run-up with paces to get a feel for conditions such as bowling downhill, uphill or into the wind.

How do I stop no-balling?

When bowlers reach the crease they take off and jump; this is called the bound. They then land to bowl; this is called the delivery stride. The bound and delivery stride tend to be of consistent length. The bowler should put a marker down where they take off from and then practise bowling. If they go past the marker, they will overstep the front line and bowl a no ball. If they want to bowl a quicker or 'effort' delivery, then they should take off slightly before the marker. This distance for the bound and delivery stride should also be measured and recorded. When marking out the run-up, don't forget to mark the take-off position. Many bowlers ask the umpire to stand level with their take-off mark to help them, an alternative is for the bowler to mark the take-off position with a line in the grass, or a small pile of sand.

Practice drills

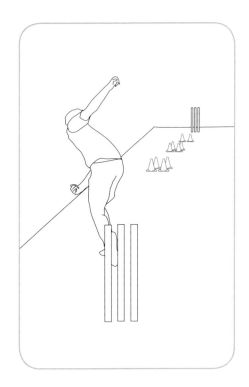

- Once each aspect of the bowling action has been practised and understood, the bowler can intensify their sessions.

- Place cones at certain lengths, e.g. for a yorker, good length and bouncer. Now practise hitting each cone in turn for an over at a time, to aid muscle memory.

- Reduce the size of the target area (good length) and get someone to plot where each delivery lands bowling six balls at a time. This replicates an over bowled.

- The bowler should focus more on where they are trying to bowl, and look at the spot on the pitch, e.g. base of the stumps for a yorker.

Problems and fixes

- *Tense gripping of the ball.* This will lock the arm from the elbow upwards. This will create little chance of swing or seam movement with a tight grip and a loss in pace. Relax the grip on the ball.

- *Running in too fast and losing front arm too early.* Rhythm is crucial and the bowler must have the right tempo through the crease for the action to work. Keep the head still and let the front arm unfold towards the target.

- *Running stride length too long in run up.* This will cause a bending of the legs during take off and delivery stride. The bowler will be unable to drive through the action resulting in a reduction in pace and a loss of height at point of delivery. Relax the stride pattern.

- *Not completing action after delivery.* This will affect movement and lead to a loss of power. The bowler must complete the action and follow-through properly.

- *Not looking at the target.* There are some who don't do this, like the England bowler James Anderson, but generally it is advisable for the bowler to keep focussing on where they are aiming to pitch the ball.

ADVANCED BOWLING

The thicker you are, the better your chances of becoming a quick bowler.
STEWART STOREY, IN FROM THE NURSERY END, 1985

Once the bowler has sorted out their action, they've got to decide how they want to bowl. If the bowler likes the idea of getting aggressive and knocking over stumps and batsmen then they'll probably want to bowl **quick**. If the bowler's body can't quite match their mind then they'll want to work on their **swing** and **seam** and accuracy to become a skilful, wily **medium pacer**. And if they like the idea of luring the batsmen to his end with **flight** and **turn** then maybe **spin** is their natural resource.

Whatever the body-shape and natural attributes of the cricketer, there will be a style of bowling that suits them. This chapter examines the different types of bowling, and the variations within them.

Stock delivery

Every bowler has a stock delivery, and it is the most common delivery a particular bowler will bowl. For example, a leg spin bowler's stock ball would be the leg break and a seam bowler's stock ball would be to hit a good length on a good line. This discipline should be mastered before any variations are explored. The stock ball should also be practised on a regular basis; the bowler should place targets on the area they wish to hit and bowl with no batsman.

If the stock ball is inconsistent, the bowler will struggle to control and contain the batsman, reducing his effectiveness considerably.

The stock ball is a bowler's most important delivery and they should have the ability to bowl it on demand.

I felt like phoning Devon Malcolm as he tried to flog the life out of the Headingley pitch, to tell him that it was the law of diminishing returns; just try to kiss the surface with the ball. Be friends and the Headingley pitch responds.

JOHN SNOW, DAILY TELEGRAPH, HEADINGLEY TEST, 1991

MEDIUM-PACE AND FAST BOWLING

In cricket, like life, everyone is different. So even though fast, fast-medium or medium-pace bowlers all operate using seemingly similar skills, there is a vast difference between the various disciplines and different bowlers.

At one end you have the brooding fast bowler, juiced on a cocktail of adrenaline and anger. At the other you have the cunning medium-pacer taking a more composed pleasure in outwitting batsmen with subtle movement off the seam or in the air. In the middle you have the fast-medium bowler who can be a mixture of both or totally his own breed again.

These stereotypes exist but there's no need to fulfil them. Every bowler will do different things. Some will take wickets through pace alone, never moving a ball off the straight in their life. Others will swing it like a Formula One driver going through a chicane. There's no one way, one action, one grip, that guarantees wickets.

So no bowler should go through this chapter thinking about what they can't do, they should think instead about what they can do and how they can add to it. It's also worth remembering that beyond all the fancy grips and variations, accuracy and consistency is a pretty decent base to start off with.

Key points for medium-pace and fast bowling

To be successful a bowler should try to work on all of these attributes:

- Pace
- Seam
- Swing
- Bounce
- Accuracy
- Control

Natural length

A bowler's natural length will be determined by their height. The taller the bowler, the shorter his natural length. A very tall bowler, for example England's Chris Tremlett at 6ft 8ins, will gain a lot more bounce from the same length than say James Anderson at 6ft 1ins because of the difference in the trajectory of their deliveries. This makes it very hard for the batsman to read and play deliveries from taller bowlers that pitch on a good length. Bounce allied to enough pace and a little movement off the seam can be enough to make a tall man a very effective Test bowler.

Natural length for fast bowlers

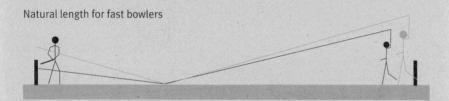

Taller bowlers

All of this makes it vital that if the bowler is tall they extract the maximum possible bounce from their action. Maximise the height by keeping the release position as high as possible (Tremlett is a good example of this). The bowler can do this by bracing the left leg on the delivery stride, maintaining a strong left arm and keeping a high head position in delivery. Conversely to Tremlett, England's Stuart Broad is an example of a tall bowler who falls away at times during the point of delivery, occasionally losing bounce and accuracy from his delivery.

Chris Tremlett (right) and James Anderson (centre) celebrate with Matt Prior (left).

Too many tall bowlers bowl too short. The tall bowler shouldn't get carried away with bowling short and making the batsman hop. **Aim to hit the top of off-stump.** Tall bowlers will get lots of wickets by virtue of the batsman's reluctance to get fully forward against the bounce. The bouncer or short-pitched deliveries should be used as a nasty surprise, not a stock delivery.

Shorter bowlers

Without the advantage of bounce, the shorter bowler's natural length will be fuller and skiddier. It's important for these bowlers to have movement in the air or off the wicket. Without the extra bounce and height the margin for error for a smaller bowler is much less and they will need to be much more skilful in their application of their stock deliveries. The smaller bowler should still use a bouncer as an effective surprise delivery, it will tend to skid on to the batsman and be difficult for them to control.

Bowling terms explained

The bowling analysis: Overs – Maidens – Runs conceded – Wickets e.g. (12–1–48–4)

Maiden: An over without a run conceded.

Average: The average number of runs that every wicket costs the bowler.

Strike rate: The average number of balls it takes the bowler to get a wicket, so the lower the strike rate the better for the bowler. A strike rate of between 40 and 60 is very good at Test level.

Economy rate: The average number of runs the bowler concedes an over, so the lower the better. In declaration cricket three runs an over is excellent, two brilliant. In one day cricket four is excellent. In Twenty20 going at six-an-over is considered excellent.

To bowl fast is to revel in the glad animal action, to thrill in physical power and to enjoy a certain sneaking feeling of superiority over the mortals who play the game.

FRANK TYSON, ENGLAND FAST BOWLER, IN 'A TYPHOON CALLED TYSON'

Pace bowling

Quick bowlers can be tall and lithe, small and barrel-like, or just really, really strong. Bowling quick is a gift, and cricket is never purer than a proper quick bowling to a gutsy batsman on a pitch that encourages both. But fast bowling isn't easy, the quick bowler must be prepared to slog their guts out on unresponsive pitches for little reward, and probably be past their best in their early 30s. There will be countless brilliant days in between, but the biggest battle for a fast bowler is sustaining their self-belief and enthusiasm during the times that nothing is going right.

In international terms a bowler would need to be bowling at around 90mph (145kph) to be considered fast, while the quickest bowlers in world cricket would be up to and over 95mph. The Pakistani bowler Shoaib Akhtar became the first bowler to break the 100mph barrier in 2002 when he was recorded at 100.04 bowling to New Zealand's Craig McMillan, while he bowled a ball recorded at 100.2mph to England's Nick Knight the following year. Neither of those Shoaib deliveries took a wicket though – proof that quickest isn't always best.

It's impossible to talk about quick bowling without mentioning the West Indies' teams of the 70s, 80s and early 90s. It's not like there weren't quick bowlers before that, it's just that no one had either had the chance or the guts to play four men bowling around 90mph in the same team. West Indies captain Clive Lloyd did, and how the rest of the world suffered – not for nothing were they known as the 'Four Horsemen of the Apocalypse'. Michael Holding, Andy Roberts, Joel Garner and Colin Croft shattered records and cheekbones in equal measure – retrospectively it seems a golden age of quick bowling but at the time opponents ran scared and journalists wrote of how the West Indian barrage was ruining the game.

Naturally those suggestions died down as West Indian dominance waned, yet while the world game was still well-stocked for quicks in the late 90s and early 2000s, recently they seem to have disappeared from the Test arena. Many reasons have been suggested – from injuries caused by too much cricket in each professional season, to hard, flat, bland pitches too suited to the batsmen, to the lure of the Twenty20 money. There is also a strong argument that it is a cyclical process, and that after a period around the turn of the century where each international side seemed to be blessed with extraordinary fast or fast-medium bowling talent (Australia – Glenn McGrath, Brett Lee and Jason Gillespie; West Indies – Courtney Walsh and Curtly Ambrose; South Africa – Allan Donald and

Shaun Pollock; Pakistan – Waqar Younis, Wasim Akram and Shoaib Akhtar; England – Darren Gough and Andy Caddick; Sri Lanka – Chaminda Vaas; India – Javagal Srinath) it was inevitable that there would be a lull.

If a bowler is lucky enough to be able to bowl quicker than other people of their age or their level, they should focus on developing that pace. Control and variation are vitally important but will come in time. Speed is money in cricket, and should be the first priority.

There is no right build to be a fast bowler, it is more important to develop the skills that make the most of the bowler's physical attributes. The tall bowler will always have a natural advantage – bounce is a hellish thing to deal with for any batsmen, so the tall quick should focus on developing a high delivery position that maximises that bounce. If the bowler is short they should get themself a good yorker and work on moving the ball in the air or off the pitch. The trajectory that a tall bowler is blessed with also makes him extremely difficult to score off – a point borne out by a glance at the career economy rates of men such as McGrath (6ft 4ins – 2.49), Ambrose (6ft 7ins – 2.30) and Pollock (6ft 3ins – 2.39), although strictly all three were fast-medium bowlers.

Like husband and wife, fast bowlers often work best in partnerships. For the tall bowler that can be working with a shorter, skiddier bowler – a dynamic that worked well for Caddick and Gough and is currently effective for the South African pair Dale Steyn and Morne Morkel. Similarly, a bowler of express pace may work best with a calmer, more metronomic presence at the other end – as it did for Lee and McGrath, Waqar and Wasim, and Donald and Pollock.

The best fast bowlers learn in time to tailor their games to the pitches they play on – some pitches will encourage genuine pace, on others the bowler will be better served keeping something in reserve and hitting the right lengths more consistently. A good economy rate is handy but strike-rate is key for the fast bowler – he is the team's spearhead, the man the captain will need to turn to when he needs a wicket, or wants to intimidate the opposition.

Finally, it's impossible to talk about fast bowling without talking about the body. If a bowler is ever going to be really fast, the chances are they're already blessed with a natural suppleness that allows their body to squeeze out those extra yards of pace. Keep working on it, the bowler must do whatever they can to stay loose-limbed. The bowler should work on core-stability and stretch like a demon to give themselves the best possible chance of avoiding the injuries that can blight a fast bowler – there is no other discipline in cricket that places such immense strain on the body, both in the run-up and delivery.

The life of a fast bowler is hard, and the bowler will have to learn to know their own body. Rarely will a fast bowler bowl without a niggle of some sort – the key is understanding when those niggles need to be attended to or rested, as there are many injuries it is not sensible to bowl through.

The 'Four Horsemen': (left to right) Andy Roberts, Michael Holding, Colin Croft and Joel Garner.

Dale Steyn (left) and Morne Morkel (right) with former team-mate Makhaya Ntini.

> **I don't really like the new Dennis Lillee. There's no substitute for bowling fast and being able to make the good players jump.**
> DENNIS LILLEE, 'MY LIFE IN CRICKET', 1982, AFTER HIS BACK INJURY HAD FORCED HIM TO SUBSTITUTE SPEED FOR SKILL

Physical, preparation, fitness

For the out and out fast bowlers it is a natural gift to be that much quicker than the rest, although there are many ways to help develop and maintain pace bowling.

- Strength and conditioning are vital throughout the year. Focus areas should be on core stability, stamina, flexibility and strength.
- Warm up and warm down before and after every bowling session.
- It is advantageous to be 'loose-limbed' and supple. This can help generate pace.
- Seek out a proper diet from a nutritionist.
- Rhythm in run up and delivery is crucial. Less effort can result in more pace.

Fast bowling directives – bowlers up to the age of 18
Injury prevention and over-bowling
Directives are now in place to protect bowlers from over-bowling at an age that could be detrimental to their long-term development and well-being. If a wicket-keeper stands back to a bowler in the same age group he would be considered as a fast bowler.

Over-bowling at a young age is a major problem. A gifted young pace bowler is wanted by everybody from school to club to county level and can end up playing far too much cricket. In the past little or no thought went into their long-term well-being.

Growth spurts need to be identified and treated accordingly. Once detected, the bowler's workload and practice should be reduced considerably during the growth period. When the body has caught up with the growth spurt then the bowler can step up their work-rate again. Another side effect to the growth spurt can be loss of coordination.

There may be no sign of injury or distress during this phase but evidence suggests that injuries manifest themselves when the bowler reaches late teens.

Directives for matches
Age	Max overs per spell	Max overs per day
Up to 13	5	10
U14 – U15	6	12
U16 – U17	7	18
U18 – U19	7	18

Directives for practice sessions
Age	Max balls per session	Max sessions per week
Up to 13	30	2
U14 – U15	36	2
U16 – U17	36	3
U18 – U19	42	3

The guidance recommends that in any seven-day period a fast bowler should not bowl on more than four days in that period, and for a maximum of two days in a row.

During a match, once the bowler has completed a spell they cannot bowl again until the equivalent number of overs has been bowled at the same end.

These directives do not apply to spin bowlers.

I just try to bore the batsman out. It's pretty simple stuff, but the complicated thing is to keep it simple.

GLENN MCGRATH, THE HUGELY SUCCESSFUL AUSTRALIAN QUICK BOWLER, REVEALS THE SECRET BEHIND 500 TEST WICKETS, 2005

MEDIUM-PACE (FAST-MEDIUM, MEDIUM FAST)

Medium-pace bowling has had a stigma attached to it – it's leading man versus best supporting actor. Everyone wants to be fast, or at least considered fast, but the vast majority can never be so. A generation of intelligent and versatile bowlers has now been labelled 'trundlers' simply because they will never bowl at 90mph.

Maybe it's because of that obsession with pace at higher levels, and the mistaken assumption that it is the only way to take wickets on flat pitches. Whatever it is, the vast majority of bowlers will never be express-quick, and no one should worry about not being so, certainly below international and professional level. Every bowling attack should have complementary skills – the medium pacer who understands his game will have the brains to provide a perfect accompaniment to the quick bowler's brawn.

What it does mean is that if a bowler cannot be genuinely quick they must develop their variations – namely swing and seam, and aspire to a consistency that few fast bowlers can match. If the bowler can master these they should be able to succeed on any wicket and in any conditions.

There are many bowlers who have been tremendously successful in international and domestic county cricket who have operated well below the 90mph barrier. Glenn McGrath is an example of this – he became Australia's second-leading wicket taker (behind Shane Warne) through a combination of bounce, the ability to move the ball off the pitch and occasionally in the air, but most importantly of all through nagging accuracy, all while bowling in the mid- to high 80s in terms of mph. These are attributes that take wickets and win matches at whatever pace and whatever level the bowler is playing at.

Finally, to re-emphasise the most important advice to the medium-pacer – know your game. The medium-pacer should know what deliveries they can bowl and what balls they still haven't perfected in the nets, and not give away runs for free. They must think about the pitch and the game situation and tailor their bowling accordingly. They will soon become indispensable to any captain.

Seam bowling

Seam bowling might appear the least glamorous of fast bowling disciplines, but it is very effective in the right conditions. It relies on two things – the prominence of the seam on the ball and the pitch. The larger the seam and the greener the pitch, the more chance an accurate bowler has of repeatedly landing the ball on the seam, and getting it to grip on, and move off, the pitch at an awkward angle for the batsman. It's a very effective form of bowling, namely because if the bowler isn't sure which way the ball will seam then the batsman will also struggle to play the delivery.

For English fans, Angus Fraser is the best example in recent times of the honest seamer. Fraser didn't really move the ball in the air, but concentrated on a nagging line and length, nipping the ball either way off the same. Consistency was key for Fraser, and in the right conditions he was a proven match-winner.

Angus Fraser was a consistent seamer for England.

The effective seamer will always be making the batsman play off-stump at just short of a good length, where batsmen have little time to react to any movement. If the ball isn't nipping, the seamer should content himself with being the bowler that the captain can rely on to stick to his line and length and provide reliability. Don't look down on that; no team will be successful without bowlers who can provide this stability.

Seam bowling can also be something for the swing bowler to fall back on if the ball isn't moving.

What it is

Seam bowling is where the ball is released with the seam in an upright (vertical) position. When it lands on the pitch it will move either in or away depending on which side of the seam is at its most prominent.

How to do it
Grip

 First two fingers close together on the seam. Side of the thumb on the bottom of the seam.

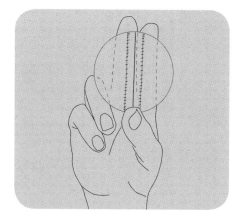

Delivery

 The wrist must stay behind the ball to allow the seam to stay upright on release.

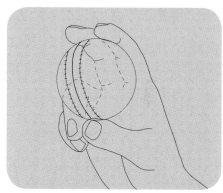

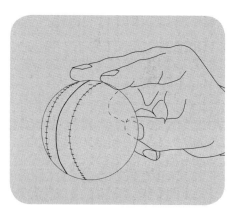 Look to maintain a high action release with a loose wrist that flicks down the seam. This creates back-spin which helps maintain an upright seam.

Slight adjustments to the seam position should be explored to see if more movement can be found.

Remember: It is important that the seam stays proud; once the seam is flattened the seam bowler's effectiveness is reduced.

Ball tampering

While a fielding side will obviously want to keep the ball in the best possible condition to swing or seam, it's important that they don't go about it illegally.

There have been several high-profile instances in the professional game of players artificially enhancing the ball's condition, either by rubbing dirt in the side of the ball to roughen its condition, picking the seam to make it more pronounced, or using illegal substances to shine one side of the ball.

These practices are against the laws and the spirit of the game and you must steer clear of all of them.

Practice drills

Using the red and white coloured ball: the bowler should work with a partner by simply throwing to each other 10-yards apart. Work on flicking the wrist to impact backspin and keep the seam upright.

Move on to bowling at targets of a good length on and just outside the off-stump line.

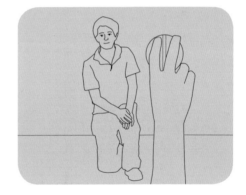

Remember the perfect length is where the batsman has limited time to react to the movement.

If the bowler is bowling with a new ball, look at its condition after every delivery; it should be possible to see a slight discolouration on the side of the seam, or some grass embedded into the seam.

If there is a larger discolouration away from the seam area, this suggests the ball is not being released in an upright position. The bowler will need to check their release position as they are missing the seam and losing the ability to move the ball off the wicket.

A high release position will result in the ball bouncing more and creating more problems for the batsman.

If the bowler's head falls away to the off-side, it will be very difficult to keep the wrist upright; focus on the head and eyes moving towards the target.

The part-time bowler

Even the batsman who bowls some medium pace should keep working on their bowling.

Paul Collingwood retired in 2011 after 68 Tests as a batsman for England. Collingwood bowled medium-pace as well, and while he took only 17 wickets in that time, his bowling was a vital part of the team dynamic. England played four bowlers for much of that period, so relied on Collingwood to bowl fill-in overs when the situation called for a change. Collingwood could bowl swing or cutters as the surface dictated, but what made him so useful to his captains was his consistency and his economy rate. As he only went at 3.20 an over, the captain could always throw him the ball and know that the opposition were unlikely to be able to go after him.

Collingwood's bowling was even more useful in the one-day and Twenty20 game, where he became one of the world's leading limited-overs all-rounders.

Paul Collingwood celebrates another useful wicket, this time against Australia in the 2010–11 Ashes.

Swing bowling

When a fast or fast-medium bowler sleeps at night he probably dreams of flattening someone's stumps with an in-swinging yorker. It's the most dramatic sight in cricket – the batsman jamming his bat down too late, the ball arcing inevitably inwards and finally the stumps flying.

Batsmen hate swing because even if they can predict it, sometimes they still can't do anything about the way the ball moves in the air. It's particularly difficult to face for a batsman who has just got to the wicket, but as a batsman if the ball is swinging it informs your every move. Every shot and every leave must now be made in the knowledge that the ball could swing back towards or away from the stumps at the last minute.

Anyone who wants to be a successful swing bowler has to gamble and be able to hold their nerve. Why? Because to swing the ball the bowler must pitch it up to the batsman, and when the ball is pitched up there is always a risk of being driven to the boundary. The risk of going for runs should not put a swing bowler off though – if the batsman is playing an aggressive shot there is more chance of deceiving them with the swing and getting them out caught, bowled or LBW.

Given that a bowling average of around 20 is considered excellent, theoretically the bowler could be hit for five fours in one over, but if they get a wicket with the sixth the bowler is still winning. Wickets are what every bowler wants, that's why the swing bowler should keep pitching the ball up.

The Pakistani duo of Wasim Akram and Waqar Younis are arguably the best practitioners of swing bowling (both orthodox and reverse) over the last 20 years of Test cricket. Their ability to move the ball late and in either direction at speeds of upwards of 90mph made them unplayable when they were in the right mood. More recently England's James Anderson has established himself as a consistently excellent swing bowler, whose impact has increased greatly since he learned to move the ball both ways, and that extravagant swing does not always get wickets. Anderson is a good model for any young swing bowler – every swing bowler needs a ball that goes the other way, and development can take time, so be patient. Anderson's unorthodox action – he looks at his feet as he delivers the ball – is further proof that there are methods beyond the textbook.

A swing bowler who can move the ball both ways can have a lot of fun. There are few better things for a bowler than setting a batsman up with four out-swingers or balls going across, and then seeing the look on his face when the bowler unleashes the in-ducker to catch him unaware.

Swing has several different forms to master – conventional out-swing or in-swing, reverse swing and even contrast swing – all of which are discussed in more detail on the following pages. It sounds complicated, but it's not. The bowler should focus on getting the right grip and a strong wrist position for delivery and watch it curve. One final thought – the closer the bowler is to the wickets on delivery the more pronounced the swing will be, and the better chance they have of getting the batsman out LBW or bowled as well as caught.

Wasim Akram (left) and Waqar Younis (right) terrorised batsmen in tandem for Pakistan.

What it is

Swing is where the cricket ball is delivered with the correct action and grip that will allow the ball to either swing in towards the stumps or away from them.

How to do it

When the bowling action is high at the release position and the seam and grip are correct, the ball will swing late. One side of the ball is shiny, the other side is scuffed up. The seam, when positioned correctly, will create a drag effect on the ball direction. This, aided by the shiny side of the ball being placed in the correct position, will allow the ball to swing.

- Develop a solid action that allows a strong wrist position on release. The release position must be strong and repeatable for consistent swing to occur.

- Have the wrist cocked but don't choke the ball (grip too tight).

- The bowler must keep the head and eyes level and focused on the area they want to pitch the ball.

- Pitch it up.

Why does a ball swing?

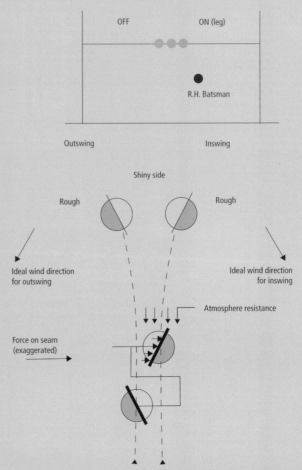

The make-up of the cricket ball enables it to swing in a unique way. Cricket balls are made of leather, coated with lacquer and hand-stitched, so when you look at a cricket ball as it swings through the air, there has to be an asymmetry about its flight (a difference between the two sides). That's why swing bowlers bowl with an angled seam, because by angling the seam the bowler affects the flow of the air on that side of the ball only.

In other ball sports it is spin that creates the asymmetry that causes balls to curve. In cricket the bowler doesn't need to create the spin, so the trick is to bowl the ball so it flows steadily along the angled seam. There is always spin imparted to the ball (with the straight arm action); the trick is to make sure it only spins along the seam.

Orthodox swing

The single most important factor in swing bowling is the release of the ball in the right orientation. If the bowler takes a brand new ball, anywhere in the world, in any weather conditions, in that first over it will swing if it is released properly.

The optimum pace for a new ball to swing conventionally is at around 70mph. If the bowler bowls quicker than this the ball will still swing, but it will be less pronounced. At a certain pace, perhaps upwards of 90mph, the ball will stop swinging conventionally and start reverse-swinging (see next page).

Perfect conditions for swing

All the bowler needs for swing is a new ball with a good seam on it. The quality of ball shows up as the bowler bowls with it over time, but they should all swing to start with. The ground conditions will play a role in how the ball deteriorates. In England the pitches are good for maintaining the quality of the ball to bowl conventional swing for a long time, as opposed to say the subcontinent, because English pitches and outfields are not as hard, dry and dusty as those in India.

There is more made out of the influence of weather on swing than is actually the case – there is no factual evidence to suggest that weather conditions have any influence on swing bowling at all. Part of it may be human nature. Observers and commentators have preconceptions that the ball will swing in overcast conditions, and don't note when it swings in sunny conditions. Even today a lot of decisions on whether to bat or bowl can be based on the weather conditions, and a lot of that is ingrained. Perhaps subconsciously the bowlers make more of an effort to release the ball well in humid, overcast conditions.

Another myth is that the bowler is more likely to swing the ball bowling into the wind. Actually, because bowling down-wind reduces the ball's speed relative to the air (a key factor in swing) the bowler is more likely to swing the ball bowling with the wind than bowling into it.

Look after the ball

Another key is to shine the ball on one side and one side only. Any bowler wants a brand new ball – it's hard, it has a nice seam and a nice smooth surface – if they can release that ball correctly it will swing. From there its a case of looking after that ball in the right way. Towards the end of the innings the bowler will want a ball where they have maintained a nice, smooth, shiny surface on one side and let the other side rough up. Assuming it has a decent seam on it, the ball can then be used to bowl conventional swing, reverse swing and even contrast swing.

Most teams now have a designated shiner or polisher – polish the hell out of it after every ball, let the other side rough up on its own. Spit and sweat are the legal ways to help polish the ball (using artificial substances like Vaseline to polish the ball is illegal and must be avoided). Early on the bowler may have to switch the side of the ball they are polishing, for example if the shiny side gets trodden on, or if it hits the boundary boards or the pitch hard and gets scuffed up. A way for a bowler to choose which side of the ball to shine is to examine the embossments on the ball; feel both sides, and if there is a difference go for the smoother side.

> *I get really annoyed with this reverse swing term. It's either an in-swinger or an out-swinger, isn't it?*
> FORMER AUSTRALIAN CAPTAIN IAN CHAPPELL REFUSES TO GET TO GRIPS WITH THE TECHNIQUE OF REVERSE SWING, 2005

Reverse swing
What it is
Reverse swing refers to the phenomenon of a ball that has been swinging one way and then starts swinging the other when the same action is used. While it might seem like a relatively recent development, it has always been a part of cricket, it is just that it is only recently that bowlers have begun to understand it and use it properly. It's very difficult for batsmen when a ball that they expect to swing one way goes the other way, making it a particularly effective delivery at the end of a one-day game when batsmen are looking to hit out.

Reverse swing has traditionally been associated with Pakistani quicks, who picked up the skill on dry sub-continental pitches where the ball wears quickly. From Safraz Nawaz in the 1970s, through to Imran Khan in the 1980s and more controversially Waqar Younis and Wasim Akram in the 1990s and early 2000s, it has proved a devastating addition to the repertoire of some already great bowlers. Younis and Akram were regarded with suspicion after they decimated England with dramatic late swing in 1992, but now the rest of the world has caught up, with reverse swing playing a prominent part in England's Ashes successes of 2005, 2009 and 2010–11.

How to do it
The key factor in reverse swing is the condition of the ball. There must be a contrast between the two sides of the ball for it to swing conventionally and then reverse – one shiny, one as dry as possible and rough, so if that's what the bowler is after they should do their best to keep all moisture off the dry side of the ball. However, if they are only after reverse swing they just need the ball to be roughed

up and have a decent seam. How long the ball takes to reverse will depend on the ball itself, the condition of the pitch, and the pace of the bowling.

Reverse swing explained

Everybody thinks there is a special way to generate reverse swing. That's rubbish. The best speed to obtain conventional swing is around 70mph, so let's say the bowler is swinging a new ball conventionally at around that pace. If the bowler were able to keep bowling without changing anything in their action, just by the face of the ball deteriorating, it would eventually start to reverse swing. The ball will reverse on its own if the ball is rough enough, which is why it's important to generate that contrast as quickly as possible. A bowler who could only bowl out-swing will find that with the shiny side facing the batsman they will get conventional swing, but if the bowler flips the ball over and bowls exactly the same delivery, it will reverse when one side of the ball has deteriorated enough. Contrast is important so that the bowler can generate both conventional and reverse swing with an angled seam and then, if the seam is destroyed, contrast swing as the bowler does not need a seam for that.

The speed at which a bowler will get reverse swing is dependent on the condition of the ball. Someone bowling at 120mph with a brand new ball would only produce reverse swing, it would not swing conventionally because of the speed. Reverse swing comes into play because as the ball roughens up, the speed at which the ball will reverse swing reduces.

Rabindra Mehta is a Sports Aerodynamics Consultant and NASA Scientist based in California

If the batsman sees the bowler is getting the ball to reverse, he may try to look at the grip as the bowler runs in to see which way the ball will swing. In this case the bowler can try to cover the ball in their run-up with their non-bowling hand.

There is no special training for reverse swing so the bowler shouldn't give up if they don't get it right straight away. Focus on bowling the ball in the right area – if the bowler can do that, the ball will be difficult to hit if it swings or not. Whether it reverses depends on ball condition and bowling speed.

Contrast swing
What it is
Contrast swing is often mistaken for reverse swing. It is swing that can be bowled without a prominent seam on the ball.

How to do it
It is bowled with the seam straight up, and can be an easier delivery to bowl than conventional or reverse swing. It has been dubbed a stock bowler's delivery, as it is achieved by keeping the seam straight and using the contrast on the sides of the ball to let the ball do all the work. This type of swing turns a seam bowler into a swing bowler too. With no seam this is the only way for a fast bowler to swing the ball.

Out-swing
- *Which way does out-swing move?* The ball will move away from the right-handed batsman towards the slip cordon.
- *What type of action is best for out-swing?* Out-swing is normally best delivered from a side-on action.
- *What length?* The ideal length for out-swing will be on a full-ish length, giving the ball most time to swing and tempting the batsman into a stroke.

 Bowler to study

JAMES ANDERSON (England 2003–)
Anderson has established himself as one of the outstanding swing bowlers in world cricket. The key is how he has improved his action. He has a higher release position and stronger wrist position than when he first came into international cricket meaning that, rather than moving the ball a long way early, he moves the ball late and just enough to catch the edge. Anderson has also added the ability to swing the ball back to the right-hander, who leave him alone at their peril. When conditions aren't in his favour, he has learned a consistent line and length that makes him a 'go to' man for his captain.

James Anderson has developed into a top-class swing bowler for England.

How to do it
Grip

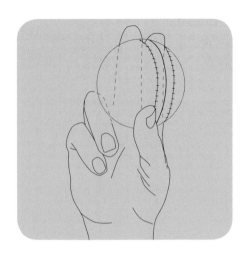

- The seam should point towards 1st/2nd slip.

- The shiny side of the ball is on the leg-side.

- First two fingers either side of the seam with the side of the thumb on the seam underneath the ball.

Delivery

- The wrist should be cocked and pointing towards the slips, while the bowling arm passes the back pocket on the left leg after delivery.

- Full completion of action is very important. The ball will swing more if the bowler bowls the ball as hard as any other delivery.

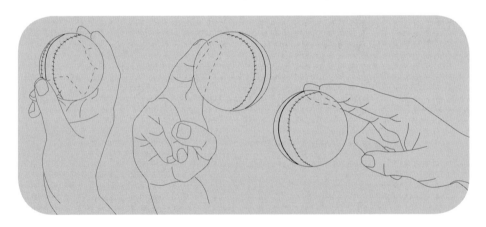

In-swing

- *Which way does in-swing move?* The ball will swing from the off-side in towards the right-handed batsman's stumps.
- *What type of action is best for in-swing?* In-swing is normally best delivered from a front-on action.
- *What length?* Like out-swing, in-swing is most effective when bowled on a full length or slightly fuller, giving the ball most time to swing.

How to do it
Grip

 The seam is positioned towards leg slip.

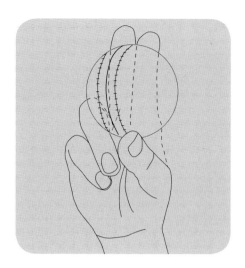

The shiny side of the ball is on the off-side and the scuffed side on the leg-side.

First two fingers either side of the seam, close together, with the flat part of the thumb on the seam underneath the ball.

Delivery

 After release the bowling arm follows through to the right leg.

 Pitch the ball up with a high action to generate late swing.

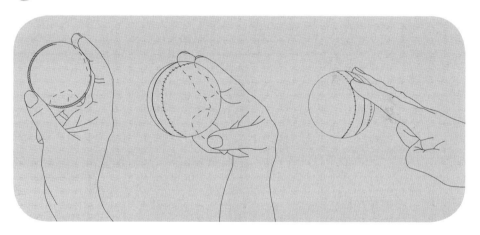

UMAR GUL (Pakistan 2003–)

Gul has a measured approach and an excellent, high head position at release putting him in the perfect place to guide his in-swinging yorkers.

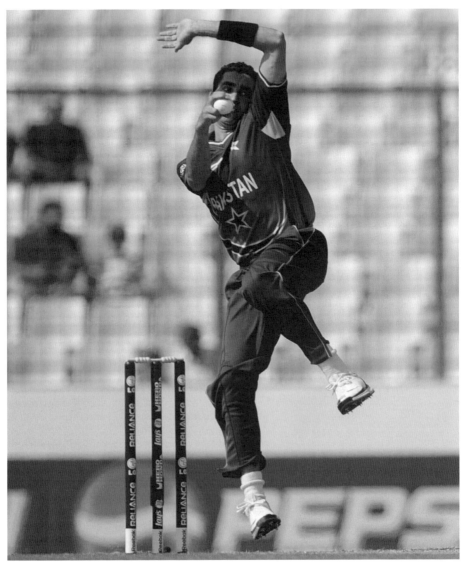

Umar Gul has been hugely successful in short-form cricket for Pakistan.

Practice drills

Using a red and white half ball, the bowler should practise throwing to a partner about 10 paces away. Work on the wrist position being at 11 o'clock for in-swing, 12 o'clock for seam up and 1 o'clock for out-swing – adjust the seam and shiny side accordingly for each delivery.

Seam position must be strong for swing to occur. The bowler must focus on keeping their fingers behind the ball.

Use an IncrediBall™ or tape up one side of a tennis ball. This will give exaggerated movement. See if it is possible to control the excessive swing by adjusting the seam position.

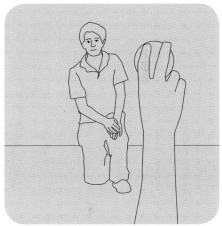

Create coloured targets slightly fuller than a good length three stumps outside off-stump for an in-swinger, off-stump and just outside for seam up, middle-to-off stump for out-swing. Now practise hitting the target area with the correct type of delivery.

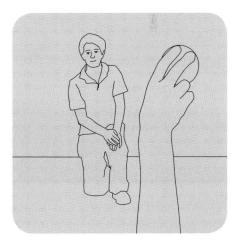

Problems and fixes

- *The ball is swinging too early.* The bowling arm may be too low at point of release. A high action brings late swing.

- *The ball is swinging too much.* Try delivering from wider in the crease.

- *Can't get it to swing.* The conditions may not be conducive to swing or the bowler might be falling away too early. Try subtle seam position changes. Make sure the grip on the ball isn't too tight. The bowler may also not be working hard enough to shine one side of the ball.

- If the bowler ever wants to stop the ball swinging, for example in one-day cricket when the ball is swinging too much, they should hold the ball across the seam.

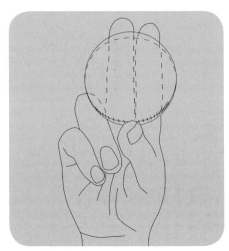

An example of holding the ball cross seam.

> **Alec rolled his fingers over the ball as he delivered it, and as it swung it pitched on the seam and became, as it were, a leg-spinner.**
> GODFREY EVANS, CREDITING ALEC BEDSER (SURREY AND ENGLAND) WITH THE INVENTION OF THE LEG-CUTTER

VARIATIONS FOR SWING BOWLERS

A bowler who can move the ball two ways is always going to cause a batsman more problems than a bowler who can only move it one way. Because it's difficult for swing bowlers to swing it both ways with the same action, many swing bowlers use cutters for their variations.

Off-cutter (out-swing)

What it is

To complement out-swing a delivery called the off-cutter is used. This is where the ball will move back into the right-hand batsman off the pitch. The off-cutter threatens the stumps so is a useful delivery in its own right, but when the batsman sees the bowler can bowl it they will be more tempted to play at those juicy out-swingers. Make sure the slips are ready for those catches.

What it does

The off-cutter moves back into the right-handed batsman off the pitch.

A: Out-swing; B: Off-cutter

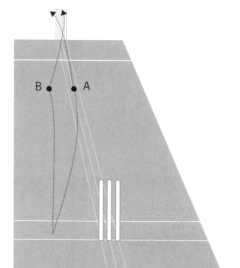

SHAUN POLLOCK (South Africa 1995–2008)
Pollock's off-cutter was teamed with away swing and an excellent bouncer. Because he got close to the stumps, the off-cutter was a very dangerous delivery in terms of its ability to trap batsmen LBW in front of the stumps.

How to do it
Grip

 Grip the ball as if to bowl an out-swinger then move the fingers so that the index (first) finger is on the seam with the side of the thumb on the bottom of the seam. Tilt the seam towards the leg side.

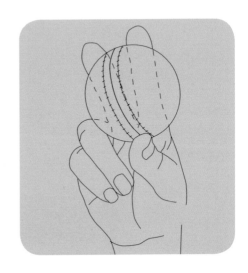

Delivery

 As the bowler releases the ball they should turn their fingers and wrist down the side of the ball similar to turning a door handle away from them in a clockwork motion.

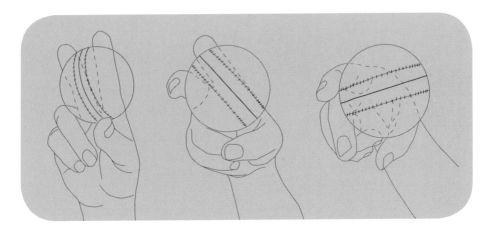

Leg-cutter (in-swing)

What it is

To complement the in-swing delivery, a ball which when pitching moves from the leg-side to the off-side is used as the main variation. This is called a leg-cutter. This is a very difficult delivery to master; it needs a very strong wrist position, so it is important to work hard on it in the nets before using in a match. When the bowler has mastered it, it is a key wicket-taking delivery, especially when teamed with the in-swinger, as it is possible to catch the outside edge of right-handed batsmen playing for the swing.

What it does

The leg-cutter pitches and moves away from the right-handed batsman, like a quicker leg-break.

A: In-swing; B: Leg-cutter

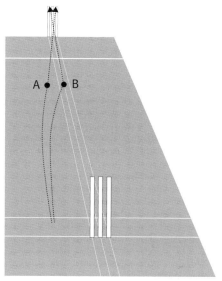

 Bowler to study

COURTNEY WALSH (West Indies 1984–2001)
By the end of his career Courtney Walsh could put the ball on a string. With an economical run-up and another excellent wrist position, Walsh's leg-cutter was a big wicket-taking delivery.

Courtney Walsh's excellent balance at the crease helped him to bowl his leg-cutter to order.

How to do it
Grip

The second finger should be placed on the seam and the flat of the thumb on the bottom of the seam.

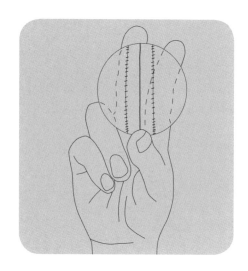

Delivery

When releasing the ball the bowler should allow the second finger to slide off the seam towards the offside. The wrist should turn in an anti-clockwise direction. Let the fingers slide down the side of the ball.

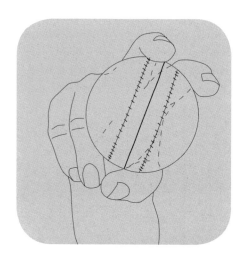
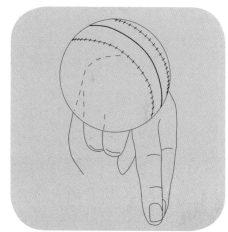

I used to give a new batsman four balls. One was a bouncer to check his courage, the second a fizzer to check his eyesight, the third was a slow'un to try out his reflexes and the fourth a bender to see if he was a good cricketer. And if he took a single off each of the four balls I knew I was in trouble.

HAROLD LARWOOD, ENGLAND FAST BOWLER, 1972

OTHER VARIATIONS

While consistency is important as a seam or swing bowler, there will be occasions when the bowler will want to employ a variation. This is anything that differs from the stock delivery, and can be a good way to try and outwit the batsman. We touched on the off-cutter and the leg-cutter earlier, used by swing bowlers to move the ball the other way. Here we will look at bouncers, yorkers and slower balls.

The bouncer

If a bowler bowls quick, then they'll need a good short ball. A good bouncer can be vital to intimidate and unsettle the batsman. It's the bowler's way of testing the batsman's bottle and heart. Is he up for the challenge?

Where it pitches

Normally about halfway down the pitch, depending on the bounce in the surface.

Who bowls it

Pace bowlers, fast-medium bowlers, maybe the medium-pace bowler as a surprise tactic.

 Bowler to study

Glenn McGrath (Australia 1993–2001)
McGrath bowled from very close to the stumps, and as a consequence his bouncer came with no angle for the batsman to use as a means of evasion. McGrath was not express pace, but by taking care not to over-use his bouncer, and focusing on targeting the batsman's throat it was an extremely effective and regular wicket-taking delivery for him.

Glen McGrath bowls a bouncer to England's Andrew Strauss in the 2006–07 Ashes.

Dangerous and unfair bowling

There are rules to stop bowlers from overdoing the short stuff. Short-pitched bowling should be used for effect, not for repeated intimidation.

(a) Bowling of fast short-pitched balls

(i) The bowling of fast short-pitched balls is dangerous and unfair if the bowler's end umpire considers that by their repetition and taking into account their length, height and direction they are likely to inflict physical injury on the striker irrespective of the protective equipment he may be wearing. The relative skill of the striker shall be taken into consideration.

(ii) Any delivery which, after pitching, passes or would have passed over head height of the striker standing upright at the popping crease, although not threatening physical injury, shall be included with bowling under (i) above, both when the umpire is considering whether the bowling of fast short pitched balls has become dangerous and unfair and after he has so decided. The umpire shall call and signal No ball for each such delivery.

From The Laws of Cricket

The best short-balls and bouncers tend to be delivered:

- **Early in the batsman's innings**. An early short-ball is a good way for the bowler to size up a batsman's technique and intention, while letting them know they face a battle.
- **From close to the wicket**. A ball that gets big on the batsman from a straighter line is much more difficult for a batsman to evade or control than one from wide of the crease which they can help on its way.
- **If the batsman is a compulsive puller/hooker of the short-pitched delivery**. Then the bowler can set a trap with two fielders at deep backward square and long leg. Delivering the ball head height or above will result in a good chance of catching them out.
- **If the batsman is committed to playing everything on the front foot**. A strategy of bowling back of a length or short may expose poor technique.
- **As part of a ploy**. Forcing the batsman back with a sustained period of bowling back of a length and short may result in the batsman having their weight more on the back foot in their set up. The odd fuller delivery (or yorker) may induce a false shot (or late on it for the yorker) as the batsman can't transfer their weight quickly enough on to their front foot. This may result in the bat face being out of control which could induce an edge behind or a chipped shot up in the air.
- **As a surprise element**. By using the bouncer sparingly the element of surprise is more likely to catch the batsman unawares and get a false shot out of them. It also sows the seed of doubt in the batsman's mind as to what the bowler is going to bowl next.
- **A nice trick** for the quick bowler to use if the batsman is ducking continually, is to bowl a bouncer while holding the ball across the seam. This will result in the ball pitching on the smooth part of the ball causing the ball to skid, and making it much more difficult to evade. Another tactic might be to bowl successive bouncers at a different pace, one slightly slower then one quicker. The West Indian Andy Roberts knocked Ian Botham's teeth out on his Somerset debut with this tactic.

How to do it

Have a slightly tighter grip on the ball than the stock delivery.

Release later (about 10 o'clock on the circle).

Problems and fixes

* *Bouncer going down the leg-side.* The bowler should check their head hasn't been pushed to the off-side. Don't try to bowl it too quickly.

* *Bowling too short.* The bowler should choose the right surface to bowl it on, and adjust their length according to the type of surface.

Practice drills

 The bowler should put cones down on different lengths and bowl to hit those lengths. Initially work on each length for a period of time.

 When the bowler moves on to bowling at batsmen in the nets, they should check with the batsman if there are any obvious signs in their approach or delivery that the ball will be a bouncer.

The yorker

The yorker is cricketing glitter. Most of the great fast bowlers of recent times have had an excellent yorker – Waqar Younis, Shoaib Akhtar, Dale Steyn, Brett Lee, Darren Gough, Shane Bond. It shows them at their best – electric pace and stumps flying.

Where it pitches

Slightly beyond the batting crease line.

Who bowls it

Any pace bowlers, particularly swing bowlers. The bowler doesn't have to be quick to bowl a good yorker but it helps.

 Bowler to study

DALE STEYN (South Africa 2003–)
Steyn is not tall by the standards of other fast bowlers, but his yorker combines speed and late movement from a lowish trajectory, making it incredibly difficult for the batsman to play.

A good yorker is:

- **Very difficult for the batsman to play** because it is so full.
- **Even more difficult to be aggressive against.** This makes it very useful at the end of a one-day innings or during a Twenty20 game.
- Useful as an element of **surprise** against top-order batsmen.
- **Always worth bowling against tall batsmen, new batsmen or tail-enders.** They may take a fraction longer to get the bat down making it an excellent attacking weapon.
- **Devastating when used in conjunction with conventional or reverse swing.** Dale Steyn, Waqar Younis and Darren Gough are fine examples of this.

How to do it

 The bowler should flick/push the wrist at the point of delivery. Try to keep a good head position at release.

Practice drills

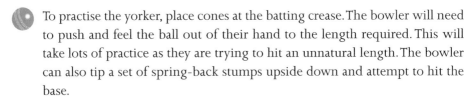 To practise the yorker, place cones at the batting crease. The bowler will need to push and feel the ball out of their hand to the length required. This will take lots of practice as they are trying to hit an unnatural length. The bowler can also tip a set of spring-back stumps upside down and attempt to hit the base.

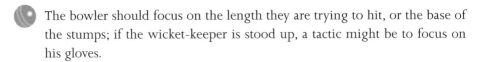 The bowler should focus on the length they are trying to hit, or the base of the stumps; if the wicket-keeper is stood up, a tactic might be to focus on his gloves.

Problems and fixes

- Bowling *full-tosses* or *half-volleys*. The yorker length is extremely difficult to hit. Some days it will click in to place, other days the bowler will find themself bowling too short or too full. The only solution is practice. Get in the nets and keep trying to hit those toes.

Slower ball

If the bouncer is brute force and the yorker is adrenaline, the slower ball is fast-medium bowler's wit.

The slower ball delivery involves the bowler looking to change his pace in an attempt to deceive the batsman into making a mistake, playing too early and hitting the ball into the air for a catching opportunity or even missing it completely, being out bowled or LBW.

Who bowls it

Any quick, fast-medium, medium-pace bowler.

Where to pitch it

Generally the bowler should aim to pitch their slower ball on a good length.

Things to remember when bowling slower deliveries:

- **The arm speed must remain consistent to the normal paced delivery**; if not the batsman will spot it early and the attempted deception will become a gift.
- **There are many types of slower balls**; bowlers should try as many as possible to discover which works best for them and then spend hours practising, firstly without a batsman before moving on to bowling in nets.
- **The slower ball is a useful weapon on early season pitches, or pitches with a lot of grass on them**. The seam will grip more in these conditions, so the ball will turn further.
- **The slower ball is also used at the end of a limited-overs game**. It creates uncertainty in the batsman's mind and prevents them from setting themselves to hit the bowler for boundaries.
- **It is good to get the slower ball up above the batsman's eyeline**. This will add to the deception, and make them think the ball is going to hit them on the full. Of course the bowler must then get the ball to come back down again!
- **The bowler should *only* try their slower ball in a match situation when they are entirely comfortable with it.**

Back of the hand
What it does
The ball goes up above the batsman's eyeline before dipping on him. It may turn, if the bowler has tried to spin it like a leg-break, or bounce higher than normal.

How to do it
 Normal grip but a little tighter, but as the bowler turns the arm over prior to release, turn the back of the hand towards the batsman on release. A difficult delivery to master, but hugely effective. The Australian Ian Harvey was a fantastic example of mastering this delivery.

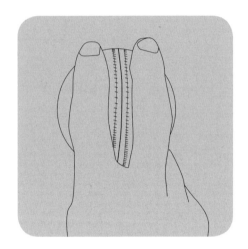

Ball deep in the hand
What it does
Because it is back in the hand the ball comes out a lot slower.

How to do it
 Normal grip, but as the arm comes over, push the ball back into the hand and grip it tightly. Maintain the normal arm speed on release.

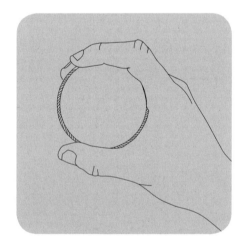

Off-cutter and leg-cutter
What it does
The ball jags off the pitch depending on which way the bowler is trying to cut it.

How to do it
 Simply exaggerate the finger pulling down (off-cutter) or pulling the finger off (leg-cutter) the ball, as discussed on pages 55–57.

Thumb from bottom to top of seam
What it does
The ball will come out slower, bounce more and impact with the wicket.

How to do it

 Normal grip but as the arm comes over on release, move the thumb from the bottom of the ball to the top. Maintain the arm speed as the ball isn't obvious to the batsman.

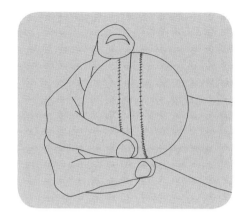

Split fingers
What it does
The ball floats down towards the batsman, possibly drifting depending on the wind or the swing on the ball.

How to do it

 Normal grip again, but at the last moment before the bound, the bowler spreads the fingers on the ball as wide as possible. They then allow the ball to go through their fingers as if they have gone through their action and left the ball behind.

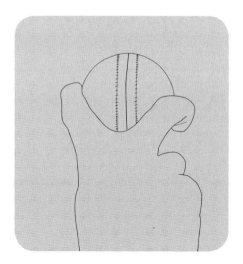

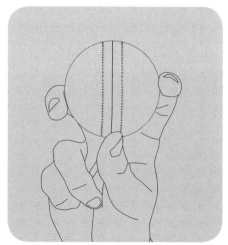

Slower ball bouncer

What this does

This appears to be a normal bouncer, but hopefully reaches the batsman after they have completed their shot, resulting in a top-edge.

How to do it

 The grip remains the same as stock delivery. As the bowler is in their bound, they take their thumb off the ball and place alongside the index finger. Rip down the side of the ball on release like an off-spinner but only use the thumb as the pressure point. Release the ball later, possibly at 2 o'clock as opposite to 12 o'clock. Maintain normal arm speed and effort.

Practice drill

 The bowler should select the deliveries they want to learn how to bowl, and get into the nets without a batsman. They should practise alternating their slower delivery with their normal ball until it becomes second nature. Only then should they start bowling at batsmen, and then take it into a game.

Problems and fixes

*   *Slower arm speed.* This gives away the attempted deception. The bowler should make sure they keep working on bowling the slower balls with their normal action.

FAST-MEDIUM BOWLING TACTICS
Opening the bowling vs change bowling
Opening bowlers

The opening bowlers are the leaders of the pack, so it makes sense that a captain will normally open with his quickest bowlers. Their role with the hard new ball is to take wickets and shape the game for the fielding side. Some will rely purely on pace and aggression while the more skilful opening bowlers will look to employ their variations, such as swing and cutters. In turn, most quick bowlers tend to love getting the new ball, because the harder it is the more it tends to bounce and swing.

The bowling order can be looked upon as a pecking order – a status symbol of the bowler's value to the captain, but the player shouldn't get caught up in that. There may be other factors involved in the captain's thinking when it comes to choosing which end a bowler will bowl from or when. Sometimes a ground will be on a slope, or there will be a strong breeze. Certain types of bowlers work better with a particular wind, while the captain may not want one of his fast bowlers wasting his energy by bowling uphill into the wind.

Opening bowlers should look to intimidate and test the batsman's technique with the occasional short-pitched deliveries, setting them up for the yorker or a full-length delivery to drive. If the bowler can get the batsman's weight on the back foot then edges are likely when they bring them forward. That said, opening bowlers quickly have to work out the right length to bowl on the surface. The most important thing for any opening bowler to remember is to make the batsman play. If the bowler doesn't do that, they have very little chance of taking a wicket, and it won't be long before the captain throws the ball to someone else.

JUSTIN LANGER'S ADVICE FOR OPENING BOWLERS

What were the most common mistakes that opening bowlers made against you as an opening batsman?

At times opening bowlers didn't make me play at enough balls. As an opening batsman it is always nice not to have to play at the new ball. The most dangerous opening bowlers were those who made you have to play every ball. Some opening bowlers also got a little carried away with saying too much. This had two advantages for me. Firstly it helped me get into the combative frame of mind so important to my batting, and secondly it became a distraction to them; taking their mind off what was most important – making me play at every ball.

Justin Langer played 105 Tests for Australia between 1993 and 2007.

Change bowling

When the openers have had their go it's the turn of the change bowlers. The role of the change bowler differs to the opening bowler in that the change bowler must be able to adapt to the situation of the game – attack if the team has taken a few early wickets, or defend if the batting side is on top.

Change bowlers tend to be less reliant on pace and so bowl to a more defensive field, aiming for a more miserly approach. They will look to bowl in partnership and stem the flow of runs at both ends; this will create pressure on the batsman and result in risks being taken. Medium pace bowlers have less margin for error so tend to be more skilful with ball movement and control (line and length). Medium pacers tend to be swing bowlers, seam bowlers or just very accurate in their execution.

Iain O'Brien on understanding your game

Accuracy is vital

It's vital when you're not extreme pace. If you're not swinging it, or moving it off the seam, then you've got to be spot on or you're going to be hurt. If you're a bit quicker, or are moving it a bit, you can get away with a little bit wayward, but the better players will still put you away. For me, I had to be as accurate as possible, because I was never a big mover of the ball. That was my main focus – to be repeatable, to try and bowl the same ball over and over again, with the bouncer every now and again.

Staying on top

The worst thing you can do is try to get the batsman out. Just keep going the same way, keep doing the things that got them frustrated in the first place. You might not always get the wicket, but you will come out of the spell knowing that you have won the little battle. The more little battles you win, the more wickets you are going to get in the long run.

Achieving consistency

To stay in the groove I needed overs, I would try and bowl 100 overs before the season started. That may not be applicable to every bowler and is not practical at every level, but the principle holds. It helped me to know that I could repeat my skills under pressure, and prepared me for bowling a lot of overs. As the season went on I always found I became more consistent, so for me it was keeping my load up. That doesn't work for everyone – injuries and fatigue affect each bowler differently.

Understand your attributes

When I first started bowling for Wellington, I was told my job would be bowling into the wind. The primary aim was not to give away runs, taking wickets was a bonus. It was the best thing for me in terms of my career, because I got good at something no one else wanted to do. When I worked that out, I embraced it and turned it into my little baby. That also helped when I was bowling from the other end, because by then the need to be consistent was ingrained in my bowling.

Sledging

An increasing trend of the modern game has been verbal intimidation of the batsman by the fielding side. This is known as sledging. There are lots of humorous examples of sledging between players, and to a degree it is part of the game. There is nothing wrong with the odd conversation between bowler and batsman, but try not to cross the line by speaking to the batsman in a way the umpire might deem offensive. This is not the way players should behave in a sport that values sportsmanship highly. Sportsmanship is defined as the conduct befitting those playing in sport, respect for one's opponent and graciousness in winning and losing. The bowler should bear it in mind at all times.

Getting into a confrontation with the batsman can also distract the bowler from their own performance. The bowler who can give the batsman a well-directed stare is a far more intimidating proposition than the one who shoots their mouth off.

Bowling to left-handed batsmen

Bowling to a left-handed batsman can be an awkward adjustment for a right-arm bowler, especially if the leftie is in partnership with a right-hander and there is frequent rotation of the strike.

Right-arm out-swing bowlers tend to bowl over the wicket to the left-hander. The bowler may explore bowling slightly wider on the crease for the delivery that is pushed across the left-hander towards the slips; the angle of the delivery creates the movement. This ball might be used to set up the batsman for an in-swinger with the aim of trapping them LBW or bowled through the gate.

Alternatively the bowler could stick to their stock delivery being an in-swinger to the left-hander, but with the occasional delivery pushed across the batsman looking for the edge.

If the bowler is bowling in-swing to a right-handed batsman it may assist them to consider bowling around the wicket to the left-handed batsman. The bowler's natural line will attack middle-and-off stump and then swing away towards the slips. To complement this form of bowling a delivery that simply holds its line will create doubt in the batsman's mind as to what they should play or leave.

Seam bowlers may bowl around the wicket and bowl leg-cutters (off-cutters to a right handed batsman) with the off-cutter or straight on delivery as the variation.

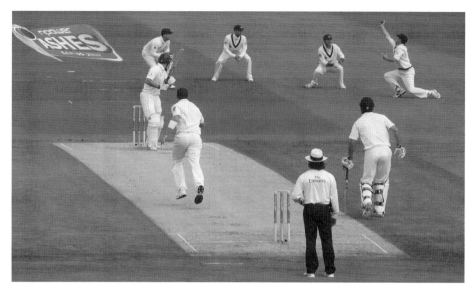

Australia's Peter Siddle finds the right line to a left-hander (England's Andrew Strauss).

Problems and fixes

- *Falling away to the left-hand side trying to push the ball across the left-hander.* The bowler should keep their head tall and their wrist strong and trust their action.

- *Struggling with line to the left-hander.* The bowler can try coming a bit wider on the crease to angle the ball across the right-hander.

- *Can't control the swing to the left-hander, or can't swing it away from the left-hander.* Try bowling with a scrambled (straight seam).

Practice drills

 Get into the nets and bowl at targets or cones set on a good line and length to the left-hander.

Using the crease and changing the angle of attack

Spin and pace bowlers should practise regularly bowling from different areas on the crease as well as bowling around the wicket. This will allow the bowler to understand the effects of changing the angle of the delivery, which can confuse the batsman. With the change of angle an edge, a misjudged leave or chasing a wider delivery may result. Using the crease effectively can be equally effective whether the ball is swinging or not. However, the variation is important if no movement is to be found in the air or off the pitch.

Bowling around the wicket

There are several occasions when the right-arm over bowler might look to come round the wicket.

An off-spinner could look to go around the wicket to a right-handed batsman if the pitch is offering turn. The same bowler might also use this tactic to a left-handed batsman so as to exploit the rough from the bowler's follow-through at the other end.

In-swing bowlers can attack the stumps far more by coming around the wicket to the right-handed batsman. The bowler can either get his prey LBW, bowled or caught behind; this greatly increases his options from bowling over the wicket.

The out-swing bowler will generally stay over the wicket to the left-handed batsman. If, however, the bowler is having limited success or is struggling with his line then a change of angle may bring a change in fortunes. The bowler can continue to use swing as the stock delivery; this should cramp the batsman up and give them little room to free their arms. The off-cutter then becomes a potent delivery. The bowler may have a strong leg-side field. By bowling wide on the crease and angling the ball into middle/leg-stump it will make life very difficult for the batsman to score through the off-side with any freedom as the angle of the ball is in the opposite direction to where they want to hit it.

Practice drill

The problems for a bowler coming round the wicket can be a difficulty in getting close enough to the stumps, and encroaching on the wicket in their follow-through.

Get in the nets and practise. The bowler should ask a friend to be the umpire, work on getting them to stand in a position they are comfortable with, and start bowling. They should mark the area of the pitch they do not want to follow through onto with cones and get into the habit of getting off the wicket in a way that does not disrupt their action.

SPIN BOWLING

A fast bowler either has the natural ability to hurl the ball down quickly or he doesn't. The reverse is true of spin bowling. I believe you can learn it from scratch.

RAY ILLINGWORTH, IN SPIN BOWLING, 1980

INTRODUCTION

A spinner reading this book will have flicked through all the quick bowling tutorials, all the eulogies to pace, bend and cut, thinking a mixture of 'hurry up' and 'what about us?!'

It's true, the spinner can sometimes be left behind amid all the talk of opening bowlers and new balls. When exactly is the spinner's turn? That depends on the captain. There is nothing strictly to say that a spinner can't open the bowling, although captains prefer to give the quick bowlers the new ball, and a shiny new ball is harder for the spinner to grip. But stay patient spinners, because when the spinner does get thrown the ball the chances are they might have quite a lot of work to do.

In international cricket, spin is seemingly constantly under threat of extinction, until a great individual comes along and re-invigorates the art. For wrist-spin that man was Shane Warne in 1992–93. For off-spin the freakish frame of Muttiah Muralitharan arrived shortly after to turn the ball in ways few believed possible (although technically also with his wrist rather than his fingers) then came Saqlain Mushtaq and Harbhajan Singh with doosras and teesras until finally in the late 2000s Graeme Swann barged in to prove that the old-fashioned skills of flight, drift and right-arm finger-spin could still win Test matches. Slow left-armers have just pottered along regardless – their natural ability to turn away from the right-hander is enough to ensure survival.

The good news for the young spinner is that in the amateur game spinners are as important than ever. With the Englishman's traditional insecurity in the face of spin bowling there are plenty of wickets to be had cheaply.

The rise of one-day cricket has led to spinners being forced to put a premium on the runs they concede, often bowling quicker and flatter at the cost of turn. But turn is like pace and swing – the spinner should seek it, cherish it and prioritise it; there is time for learning control later. Without these attacking weapons, the spinner will do well to be more than someone the captain throws the ball to when they want to tie an end up.

The captain plays an important part for any spinner. The spinner seeking to turn the ball and give it flight is going to go for runs on occasion, and a wise captain will know this, set the right fields and be patient. A bad captain will tell their spinner to bowl flatter or take them off after an expensive over. The spinner should get used now to the fact that there will be times when they are badly captained. It's up to the individual to retain their self-belief and keep trying to turn that ball.

> **I am not unhappy to be hit for six sixes. I want batsmen to play shots. Only then can I get them out.**
> BISHAN BEDI, INDIAN LEFT-ARM SPINNER

What makes a successful spinner

The young spinner will encounter numerous problems throughout their development. Perseverance and a big heart will take a spinner a long way.

Key points for the spin bowler to consider are:
- **Learn to spin the ball hard** then work on control.
- **Talk** to experienced spinners, pick their brains for advice.
- **Love to bowl** and don't be afraid to practise alone (with targets etc).
- Start practising variations when comfortable with the action but always finish the session with the **stock delivery**.
- **Read** as many coaching books and autobiographies as possible. Learn the game.
- Once the spinner has learnt to spin the ball they should focus on **consistency** and work on developing **control**. If they can bowl well to their field, the batsman will have to take risks to score runs.
- **Be patient** – if the ball isn't spinning they can still deceive the batsman through subtle changes of pace and use of the crease.

- **Be positive** – always look to attack. Get the ball above the batsman's eyeline.
- Don't bowl at the bat. Make the **bat find the ball**.
- **Start and finish the over well** (dot balls). This creates pressure and keeps the spinner on top.
- Spin bowling is like a game of chess. **Outwit** and plot the batsman's demise.
- Always look to **improve**.
- Control the controllables – and focus hard. **The spinner shouldn't allow external issues to cloud their mind.**
- The spinner should know their own **game-plans**.
- **Be aware of the conditions**. Which way is the wind blowing? How will that affect the bowling? Is there any rough to aim at?
- If the spinner is bowling on a turning wicket they should be patient – **don't expect to run through the opposition.**

What it is

The main objective when trying to bowl spin is to bowl the ball with as many revolutions (rotations) on the ball as possible, so that when it lands on the pitch it will deviate. The more revs, the bigger the spin.

The delivery is a lot slower than the fast or medium-paced bowlers. Spinners tend to come into their own as the game develops and the state of the surface deteriorates. This will allow the seam to purchase on the loose surface and impact more spin and uneven bounce.

There are two main types of spinner – the finger-spinner and the wrist-spinner. As the names suggest, finger-spinners (or orthodox bowlers) impart spin on the ball using their fingers as the ball leaves the hand, while wrist-spinners try to impart turn on the ball by twisting their wrists at the point of delivery.

The stock deliveries for the main forms of spin are as follows:

Right-arm

- **Off-spin**: right-handed bowler classed as a finger-spinner and will turn the ball from off-stump to leg against a right-hander.
- **Leg-spin**: right arm wrist-spinner where the ball will turn from leg-stump to off.

Left-arm

- **Left-arm orthodox**: finger-spinner who will spin the ball from leg to off-stump to a right-handed batsman.
- **Left arm unorthodox**: left-arm wrist-spinner. Aims to turn the ball from off-stump to leg to a right-handed batsman; this delivery is called the Chinaman.

EXPERT COACHING TIP

Each type of bowler will have variations to their stock delivery. When it comes to learning spin bowling, 'reverse chaining' is an excellent way to pick up the basics. That is starting from a static position or base, followed by a step into the action and, when the spinner is comfortable with those, then mastering the run-up into the action.

It's imperative for the younger spin bowler, when working on static and step-in routines, not to be forcing the ball down the required distance as their lack of strength will affect their action. Take the stumps away, do it anywhere over any distance, just practise spinning the ball.

Shane Warne walked up to bowl, but he had strong shoulders and drive enabling him to send the ball down with vicious turn. For young or inexperienced bowlers, a run-up is key to getting momentum through the crease and aiding their ability to have a repeatable action allowing most spin.

Key points

Deceive the batsman with subtle changes of pace/line of delivery/type of delivery/spinning hand/arm ball/top spinner/variations.

Flight – get the ball above the batsman's eyeline, this will deceive the batsman in the length of the ball.

Explore lowering the arm position on release; if the bowler delivers from a high arm (12 o'clock), they should try a lower angle (10 o'clock) release. This will change the flight and the amount of spin on the ball.

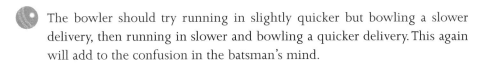 The bowler should try running in slightly quicker but bowling a slower delivery, then running in slower and bowling a quicker delivery. This again will add to the confusion in the batsman's mind.

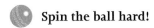 **Spin the ball hard!**

KEY TERMINOLOGY

Flight
The path of the ball. The aim for the spinner is to get the ball up above the batsman's eyeline and down again. If there is spin and drift on the ball this can be very difficult for the batsman to play.

Drift
If the action is good, the ball will drift/swing the opposite direction to how it will turn when it bounces.

Bounce
If the bowler hits the seam the ball will get extra bounce. This can be useful for the spinner, especially if the batsman is playing on the front foot.

Turn/Spin
What the ball does if the spinner puts plenty of revolutions on the ball and it hits the seam. What every spinner is trying to do.

> *The great spin bowlers were personalities and men of character – not always pleasant but invariably interesting. They may have lacked the charm and friendliness of their faster confederates; they may have been more temperamental and less self-disciplined; but there seemed to be an absence of orthodoxy about them and they were able to meander through life as individuals not as civil servants.*
> ARTHUR MAILEY DISCUSSES SPIN BOWLING

> When you're an off-spinner there's not much point glaring at batsmen.
> If I glared at Viv Richards he'd hit me even further.
> DAVID ACFIELD, ESSEX SPINNER, 1982

Deliveries and flight for off-spin

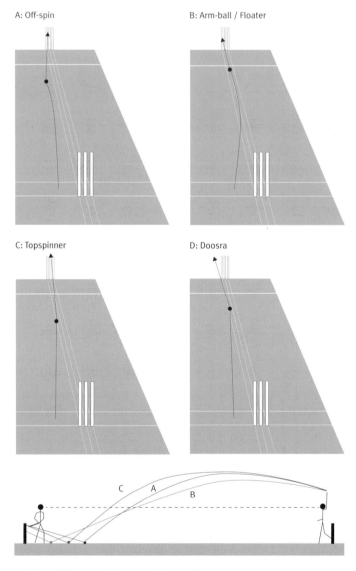

A: Off-spin *(NB: Doosra follows same flight as off-spin)*
B: Arm-ball
C: Topspinner

OFF-BREAK/FINGER-SPIN

An English cricket fan in the 1990s could have been forgiven for giving up on off-spin as a means of troubling good batsmen. Peter Such, Mike Watkinson, Shaun Udal, Robert Croft – excellent, resourceful county cricketers all, they were unable to consistently influence games at Test level. Off-spinners are denied even the angle and turn away from the right-hander that their left-arm, finger-spinning counterparts enjoy. Set their struggles against the prodigious and dramatic turn of Shane Warne's leg-spin and the future seemed doubly bleak.

Yet while English off-spinners struggled, in the Indian sub-continent bowlers were busy developing new deliveries to reinvent off-spin. It worked – not since leg-spin in the 20s and 30s has a craft developed as much as off-spin has since the mid 90s. At the forefront was the doosra – the one that goes the other way, giving the off-spinner vital variation and enabling him to beat the right-hander's outside edge. The doosra could date back as far as the West Indian Sonny Ramadhin in the 1950s, but has been credited to the Pakistani Saqlain Mushtaq in the 1990s. Other bowlers soon caught on – including India's Harbhajan Singh, while Sri Lanka's Muttiah Muralitharan, now retired after becoming the first bowler to reach 800 Test wickets, is perhaps the most famous and dramatic exponent of the delivery. While he turned the ball in the direction of an off-break Murali was technically a wrist-spinner with a very unusual action, and it meant he got tremendous revs and turn on his doosra.

The rise of 'mystery' spinners like Muralitharan was a trend that has made all the more unlikely the more recent success of the England spinner Graeme Swann, who boasts no magical variation, but a hefty dose of spin, flight, drift and gumption, not to mention a tendency to attack the stumps. Swann's success is proof that there is no single way to succeed in cricket, but the bowler has got to give themselves a chance. That's why, even in off-spin, one of the more conservative forms of bowling, any young cricketer should concentrate on developing the skills to take wickets and be an attacking option for his captain.

What it is

This ball will turn from the right-hander's off-stump towards the leg-side.

How to do it
Grip

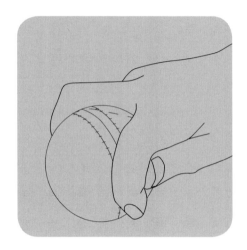

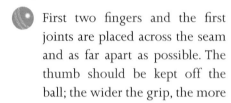 First two fingers and the first joints are placed across the seam and as far apart as possible. The thumb should be kept off the ball; the wider the grip, the more potential for spin.

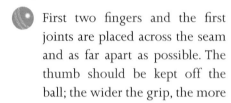 Young bowlers may have small fingers so another grip to try is to place first fingers alongside the seam with the other down the side of the ball.

Release

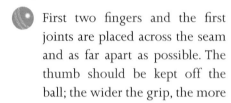 In order to spin the ball, pull down on the first finger release. On release, the wrist should turn in a clockwise direction as though opening a door. Work hard on the first knuckle joint of the index finger during release.

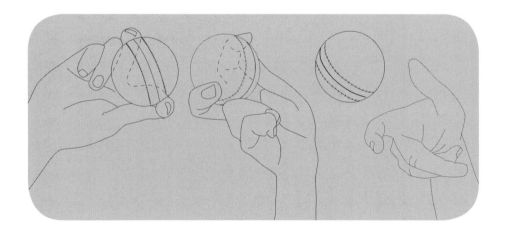

Action

In a standing position align the hips and the shoulders toward the target. The back foot should be parallel to the crease with the front foot pointing towards fine leg.

Take a small delivery stride. Look behind the front arm while gathering the ball by the side of the chin. The bowler should be bowling against a braced front side, with their hands gathered in front and their weight forward.

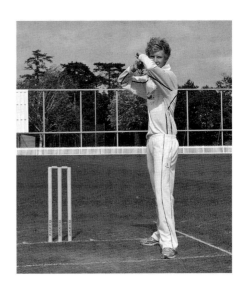

Land on the ball of the foot; this will allow the bowler to pivot, while the back leg drives through close to the front leg. Keep big circles with the arms and keep everything close to the body.

Stay tall on release of the ball. Follow through and complete 180 degrees pivot with the head and eyes remaining still.

Add a run-up

After plenty of practice, the bowler can now introduce the run-up and approach to the crease.

The approach to the crease is short in length but must still have rhythm. It should be smooth with a slight acceleration into the bowling action and the head and eyes still and level throughout. Many off-spinners like to have a curved approach which allows them to get into a side-on position more easily. The landing position should be mid-crease to get close in to the stumps. From close in to the stumps a big spinner of the ball would look to curve the ball away and spin the ball back into the batsman.

Challenging drill

Whenever possible a spinner should try to practise with a red and white ball (half and half). This a fantastic visual aid for the spin bowler – if the two colours stay constant until it pitches, this indicates a good grip and a strong chance of imparting spin.

- Work with a partner 10 feet apart; throw a tennis ball to each other bouncing once. Emphasise the index finger working down the ball to enable the ball to spin. Use a line in a sports hall or a piece of string for a visual aid and line.

- From the static position, move back and introduce a run-up, again using the line or rope as a visual guide.

- Place cones into a target area according to the type of spinner, e.g. outside off-stump to spin in for the off-spinner, middle and leg-stump for the leg-spinner and left arm orthodox.

- To encourage flight (getting the ball above the batsman's eyeline), tie a rope two-thirds of the way down the pitch just above head height. Then place cones in a box shape on a good length. The bowler has to get the ball up and over the rope but land it in the box and spin the ball. The ball must be delivered with energy.

- If no rope is available, a group of three can work together. One player stands in the middle two-thirds down the pitch, while the other two bowl over the first's head and into the box; for this drill, use the soft IncrediBall™ and possibly ask the man in the middle to wear a helmet.

Quicker deliveries: with the rope still in place, try to bowl under the target; this should be a quicker and flatter delivery. Get a partner or coach to stand at the batsman's end. The bowler should now try both disciplines of bowling over and under the rope; asking the coach or partner to call out what they think they have bowled. The bowler is trying to deceive and confuse the batsman so vary the speed of approach to give them no obvious signs of what delivery is coming.

Off-spin drill

Place a stump on a good length outside off-stump (depending how big a spinner the bowler is). Bowl to the off-side of the target and spin it back looking to hit off-stump.

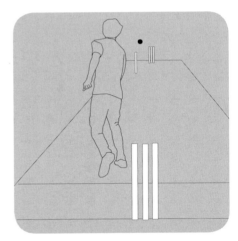

If the action is good the off-spinner may bowl with drift that moves the ball in the air from leg towards off. Introduce another target stump. The stumps are almost in a straight line. The bowler must drift the ball past the first stump and then spin the ball hard past the second one and on to the stumps.

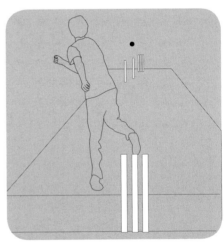

Spin the ball from hand to hand. Whether off-spin or leg-spin, try the different grips and variations. Flick from hand to hand; this will help the bowler get used to the different grips and have a better feel for what they are doing.

Problems and fixes

- *Not completing the action.* This will mean no revolutions or turn. Put energy into the delivery.

- *Bowling with a wet ball.* Struggling to grip the ball with a wet seam. Narrow the grip, and try to spin the ball using the wrist.

- *A cut finger.* Unfortunately this is just part of the job from bowling a lot with a hard seam. The bowler should inform his captain if he is struggling to grip the ball properly.

- *Weak front arm.* Doesn't drive the bowler through their action, so the ball will spin less. Keep the left-arm strong.

VARIATIONS FOR THE OFF-SPINNER

Given that the conventional finger-spinner is rarely a huge turner of the ball unless on a particularly helpful wicket, it's important that they possess some variation to help keep the batsman guessing. Of course, the off-spinner should always look to vary their flight, pace and angle on occasion, but there are other ways to sneak past the batsman.

Some are harder to learn than others. The doosra has become something of a modern phenomenon, but is incredibly difficult to bowl legally. If the bowler can't manage that, there are more conventional ways to deceive the batsman. They're all outlined below.

The arm-ball (floater)

What it is

Essentially a gentle out-swinger, a very useful delivery to batsmen who are trying to sweep.

What it does

This delivery will move from the leg-side to off-side in the air, and then doesn't turn back.

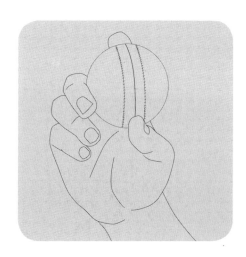

GRAEME SWANN (England 2008–)
Swann's arm-ball is very well disguised, but he doesn't overuse it, maximising its effect.

Graeme Swann in action for England.

How to do it

 The seam must be placed in an upright position with the first finger on the seam and the second finger is some way down the ball, and the thumb on the bottom of the seam. Deliver with the grip shaping the ball to the off-side.

 This delivery could be used against a right-handed batsman who is sweeping. Bowl it full length and slightly quicker resulting in a good chance of LBW. This ball should be used sparingly.

Top-spinner

What it is

This is a ball to distort the batsman's perception of length; very useful if they are coming down the wicket.

What it does

The ball dips in flight and lands shorter than anticipated, before bouncing higher than usual.

How to do it

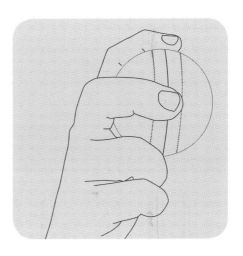

 Release from a higher position over the top of the fingers with the seam going straight down the pitch.

Doosra

What it is

A highly controversial delivery either introduced or reintroduced into the game in the 1990s by the Pakistani bowler Saqlain Mushtaq. The name 'doosra' literally means 'the other one' in Urdu. A fiendishly difficult delivery to pitch correctly, Saqlain himself said it took two or three years of practice before he trusted himself to bowl it in a match.

What it does

This delivery turns from leg towards off-stump.

How to do it

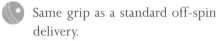 Same grip as a standard off-spin delivery.

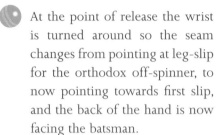 At the point of release the wrist is turned around so the seam changes from pointing at leg-slip for the orthodox off-spinner, to now pointing towards first slip, and the back of the hand is now facing the batsman.

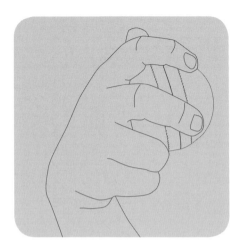

Use the fingers to spin the ball as normal and turn the wrist clockwise, and release the ball out of the back of the hand.

Bowler to study

Saqlain Mushtaq (Pakistan 1995–2004)

Saqlain Mushtaq says, 'With my offie I roll my fingers over the ball towards the batsman using two fingers to impart the spin. With my doosra, I lock my wrist with the back of the hand facing the batsman, then use three fingers to spin the ball. My wrist still rotates towards the batsman but the ball spins the other way. My grip does  not change and neither does my action. If you are trying to learn to bowl a doosra, don't give up – it is very difficult but you'll get used to it. To practise, stand a short distance from a wall with a tennis ball and throw doosras at the wall. Don't use your proper action; get used to the ball releasing correctly so your hands and wrist know what a doosra feels like, then move backwards and finally start using your action.'

This interview originally appeared in the Wisden Cricketer

Caveat

Bowlers have had problems bowling the doosra legally due to the big bio-mechanical change in a bowler's action, with bowlers accused of illegally straightening the arm at the elbow at the point of delivery. This is a fun ball to be explored, but takes years to evolve.

Practice drill

 Use the red and white ball and bowl to a partner 10 feet away. The bowler can then progress to nets but shouldn't bowl at a batsman until they have mastered the technique.

Mushtaq Ahmed on bowling spin

The key point is to see the limitation of the spinner. Encourage young spinners to learn to spin the ball. You don't want to change bowlers too much later in their career; you want to encourage them to spin the ball as much as they can early on.

If a bowler turns the ball then later on they can work on line and length. The inexperienced spinner shouldn't worry about the consequences too much. As a spinner you can't bowl yorkers or bouncers, you have to have a strong temperament. I always use the phrase, 'You can hurt my bowling, but you cannot take my smile away from me'. Play your cricket and enjoy it.

Common mistakes are not to have a repeatable action, and to be happy to become a container rather than a match-winner. The spinner has to come out of their comfort zone and learn to spin the ball. For three or four weeks it might not feel right, but one day it will click, and the ball will turn more and more. Sometimes bowlers are scared when success is not immediate and worried about being criticised by their coaches and teammates. Don't be stuck in your comfort zone.

A spinner should always be prepared to go for runs. The batsman is going to come at them, but that's why spinners win matches – they take key wickets.

A captain has to understand the spin bowler. How to adjust the field, if they're not bowling well when to withdraw them and when to bring them back. Spin bowlers need to be handled right.

I always believed that today the batsman hit me for five fours but maybe I'll take a wicket with the sixth ball. One wicket can change everything. I used to think that and really mean it. That belief is key. Often if young bowlers get hit for a couple of sixes their heads drop and they worry about being taken off. Keep believing in yourself. **Believe you are a match-winner**, and imagine good things. Visualise yourself taking wickets. Whatever you imagine, your body will act out. If you have a bad day, be honest with yourself, but recognise that tomorrow is another day, and can be your day.

In one-day cricket the temptation is to bowl flat and contain the batsman. But if you can turn the ball in Twenty20 or one-day cricket you have a better chance to be successful because you can take wickets. Bowl your natural length for declaration cricket, don't try and bowl yorkers. You already have fielders out on the boundary, back yourself that if you bowl the right ball the batsman is going to have to work very hard to hit you for six.

Mushtaq Ahmed played 52 Tests for Pakistan between 1990 and 2003

Deliveries and flight for leg-spin

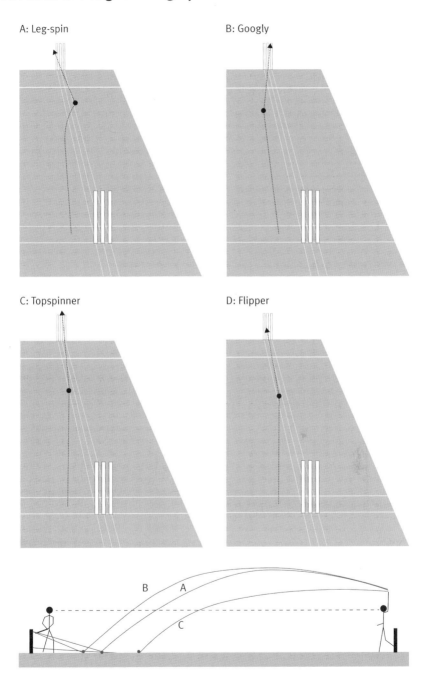

A: Leg-spin

B: Googly

C: Topspinner

D: Flipper

A: Leg-break *(NB: Googly also the same length)*
B: Topspinner
C: Flipper

I remember playing in dozens of matches with Douglas Wright when he should have never been in the side. Not only did we find ourselves playing with ten men, but with every over of honest toil he was driving another nail into our own coffin.

<small>COLIN COWDREY, KENT TEAM-MATE, ON THE PERILS OF WAYWARD LEG-SPIN</small>

Leg-break/wrist-spin bowling

Fast bowlers run in hard, pull lots of stupid faces and try to hurt people. Spin bowlers hop, skip or walk in, and beat the batsman with their mind. Off-spin is a noble and rewarding pursuit. Leg-spin is the witchery of cricket.

An international leg-spinner needs to have a multitude of deliveries (some made up), they need to deal with big bats and ever-encroaching ropes, their technique is super slowed down until the batsmen sees all their tricks and then they are expected to drop the ball on a good spot from the back of their hands. There is a reason that few make it to the top level. Leg-spinning is by far the hardest, least understood and most complicated art in cricket. Captains don't understand it, commentators are obsessed with it, and leg-spinners are still the least common bowlers in world cricket.

That wasn't always the case; in the past, even teams like South Africa would have up to four in their line-up. Australia would regularly have two for years, and Pakistan have rarely had a leg-spinner out of their side. In the 80s it seemed that Abdul Qadir, the charismatic twirly-armed genius from Pakistan, was keeping the art alive on his own; he was the leg-spinning dodo bird. Qadir was loved by the purists but his record was far from awe-inspiring. With the West Indies not even thinking of a spinner, let alone a leg-spinner, and other sides preferring safe finger-spin options, it looked like leg-spin may be slipping from the game.

Then a tubby Victorian with badly peroxided hair won a game in Sri Lanka. Then won a game in Melbourne. Then bowled Mike Gatting with a delivery that has been replayed almost as many times as the moon landings, and from then on Shane Warne brought leg-spin back. At the same time Mushtaq Ahmed, Abdul Qadir's understudy, was also showing people what could be achieved with sleight of hand and a cheeky disposition. Warne took leg-spin from a secret passed from mostly Indian, Australian and Pakistani players, to the big screen. Alongside Warne and Mushtaq was Anil Kumble, Shahid Afridi, Paul Strang, Paul Adams, Stuart MacGill and a host of wannabes all over the globe, leg-spin was now seen as a major part of cricket again.

The top leg-spinners have similarities, and very little of that has to do with how they bowl. To be a leg-spinner the bowler needs to believe in themselves far more than any other cricketer. Listen to any contemporaries of Warne or Qadir and you'll find that it's their amazing self-belief that keeps them going. A leg-spinner can bowl the best ball of their life and still be slogged over mid-wicket. Most people get disheartened with this – Warne and Qadir made batsmen think that the shot was part of their plan when it was anything but.

If a bowler can spin the ball, which is not even a pre-requisite (as Anil Kumble showed), and wants to become a leg-spinner, they'll need a cricket ball. Not one to use in the nets, but one to hold at all times. To flip between hands on the way to school, while watching a film, while waiting for dinner to be ready. A leg-spinner must feel like the ball is an extension of their hand, because they aren't bowling it with a safe seam up position: it will be coming out the back of their hand every ball, and that is the hardest part to master. If they get it right, there isn't a cricket team in the world that won't have them.

Fast bowling may be fun, but there are few things in cricket more satisfying than hopping in off a couple of paces to totally confuse a batsman.

What it does
Against a right-handed batsman a leg-break will turn from leg-stump towards the off-stump.

Key points

 Leg-spinners more so than off-spinners are slow developers. Persevere and do not be too disheartened when things go wrong.

 No bowler can be a part-time leg-spinner.

 Too many leg-spinners disappear between the ages of 15 to 17. This is often due to unsympathetic coaches/captains. Don't give up.

How to do it
Grip

 The first two fingers (joints) are placed along the seam. Keep the third finger bent and lying alongside the seam. The thumb may rest on the ball but plays no part in the spinning process.

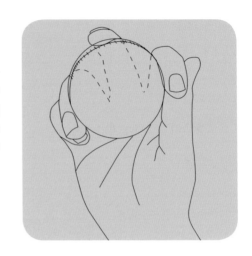

Release

 On release keep the wrist cocked, as the third finger and knuckle imparts the spin. Full follow-through. Spin the ball up during delivery, with the back of the hand towards the face on release. The bowler should imagine reading the time on a watch.

Leg break action

From a static start keep the back foot parallel to the crease, with the hips and shoulders also aligned. The front foot should be pointing to leg slip.

This delivery needs a longer delivery stride than the off-spinner. Look behind the front arm, while keeping the ball-carrying hand forward with the wrist cocked. (Leaning forward in the gather.)

The head and eyes should be level and focused on the target. The non-bowling arm starts coming up and moves towards the target, while the front leg braces as the arm comes over to bowl, allowing the bowler to be tall on release.

As the bowler is about to bowl, the shoulders tip up and over, not across. The back leg and hip drive forward with the right hip finishing down the wicket at the target.

Keep the wrist cocked on release. At 1 to 2 o'clock, release. A full swing of the arms to help complete the follow-through and finish in the fielding position (body front-on at the target ready to receive any strokes back up the pitch).

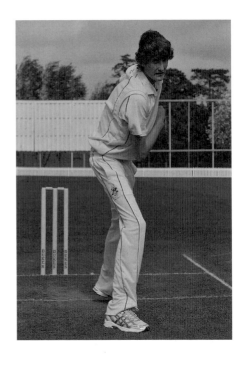

Run-up

Leg-spinners have a short run-up but it must have plenty of energy. A slight curve will enable the bowler to get into the side-on position more easily, with a good rhythm allowing the action to function when in the delivery stride. It is important to stay well balanced throughout.

Terry Jenner on leg-spin

For wrist-spinners to be successful you have to accept batsmen will score runs off them. If you are not willing to give runs away you will retard the development of the spinner. They are encouraged to bowl it faster and flatter and that usually costs them any spin they've got. The most difficult part of the art is to become accurate and maintain your spin, which is why leg-spinners mature in their mid-20s or later. Not even Shane Warne matured at 22.

Confidence plays a key role in the development of spinners. Be patient.

One thing with Warne, through all the changing body shapes, you can never see the size of his heart. If you are going to be as good as Warne you have to have courage – he's been hit for more sixes than any other bowler.

Terry Jenner was Shane Warne's mentor. He died in 2011 aged 66. This interview originally appeared in the Wisden Cricketer

Practice drill for leg-spin

 Underarm flicks to a partner about 10 feet away (bouncing the ball once). Work on rotating the wrist and spinning the ball. Now incorporate the back leg driving through during release, to get the hips and the arms driving through hard. Move on to bowling in the nets using targets instead of a batsman.

Problems and fixes

*   *Pushing the ball down the leg-side.* The bowler may be trying to spin the ball too hard, and losing the left-arm (or guider) early.

*   *Bowling full tosses.* If the bowler's left arm isn't driving them through they may release too early and bowl full-tosses.

Dragging the ball down. If the bowler is too tense in their action they may release the ball too late and drag the ball too short.

If the front foot gets too far across for the leg spinner it can cause difficulties in transferring the bowler's weight through the action. It could also cause the bowling arm to release the ball too upright (vertical) and spinning variation will be affected.

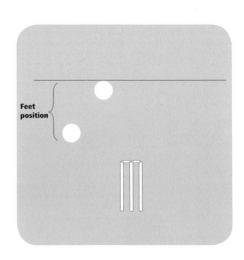

Feet position

Gone are the days when you bowled leg-spin at an Englishman and he just fell over.
Paul Strang, Zimbabwe leggie, during his first season in county cricket, at Kent, 1997

> *Poor old googly! It has been subjected to ridicule, abuse, contempt, incredulity and survived them all.*
> B.J.T. Bosanquet, inventor of the googly, 'Wisden', 1924

Leg-spin variation – googly

What it is

A great delivery for the leg-spinner against the left-hander, or an excellent delivery to a right-hander who is leaving the leg-break well.

What it does

The googly spins from the off-side to leg for a right-handed batsman.

How to do it

- The grip is identical to that of a leg break, the major difference being the hand position on release.

- The back of the hand faces the batsman; this puts the seam position pointing towards fine leg. The release position can be slightly higher than the leg break.

- During release, the bowler pushes their little finger in the direction of the intended spin.

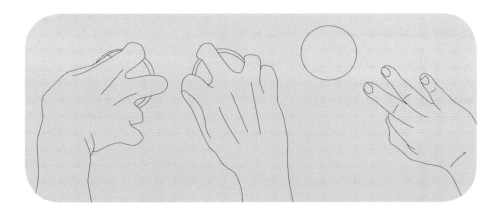

Bowler to study

ANIL KUMBLE

Kumble's stock ball was actually the googly – he bowled the leg-break as a variation. It didn't stop him taking 619 Test wickets, hurrying the ball on to the batsman from a bouncing approach to the crease.

Max Waller on the mental side of the game

The mental side of the game is as important, if not more important than the technical side of the game. Working with Murali Kartik and Saqlain Mushtaq at Somerset they always say the key attribute for a spinner is confidence, and belief in yourself and what you are doing. I was lucky enough to work with Shane Warne in a masterclass at the Oval on the final day of the Ashes test in 2009. His incredible self-belief still shone through, a self-belief that helped him be one of the greatest bowlers of all time.

Max Waller is a leg-spinner on the Somerset staff, he was coached by Mark Davis at Millfield School

Top spinner

What it is

As with the off-spinner, this is a ball to deceive the batsman in the flight, great against those who want to use their feet.

What it does

The top-spinner dips earlier than the batsman expects and bounces higher than normal. The seam rotates towards the batsman.

How to do it

 The top-spinner also has the same grip as the leg break. The position of the seam on the release is at 12 o'clock, and the bowler should look to spin the ball up and over to create the over spin.

Flipper

What it is

Shane Warne was deadly with this delivery in his early career. It creates the impression of being a long hop before skidding on sharply to hit the batsman on the pads.

What it does

The flipper curves in towards the batsman and skids off the surface. It is usually deliberately pitched shorter to deceive the batsman.

How to do it

 The grip changes. The thumb is placed underneath the ball on the seam with the top two fingers on top of the ball, across the seam. During release, the fingers flick or push the ball towards the target. This creates the backspin on the ball. The shiny side of the ball is facing the off-side to assist the drift in to the right-handed batsman.

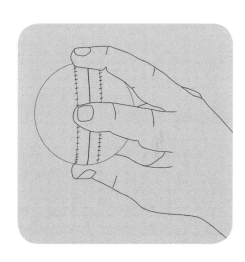

EXPERT COACHING TIP

When practising your variations it is important to keep working on your stock ball too.

LEFT-ARM SPIN

Left-arm spinners are a valuable rarity in cricket. The change of angle always makes them an attractive option for a captain, whichever way they then look to spin the ball. There are two main types of left-armer, the left-arm orthodox (or slow left-arm) and the imaginatively named Chinaman bowler.

> *Mentally, my stock ball pitches leg and hits off.*
> PHIL EDMONDS, ENGLAND SLOW LEFT-ARMER, IN 'A SINGULAR MAN', 1985

Left-arm orthodox

Slow left-armers are finger-spinners too, but they've always been the off-spinner's better-looking cousin because of their natural ability to turn the ball away from the right-handers.

Like left-handed batsmen, for some unspecific reason, slow left-armers are stereotyped as possessing a laconic grace. From the West Indian great Sir Garfield Sobers, through Bishan Bedi and the enigmatic Phil Tufnell to Daniel Vettori, who has underpinned the New Zealand team for the past decade – it just looks easier when it's done left-handed. In reality, for every Vettori there is an Ashley Giles, and the two make interesting counter-points for the left-armer's main skills.

Vettori is a bowler of flight and guile, who gets the ball up above the batsman's eyeline and spins it hard from over or around the wicket. Giles was a converter seamer who, despite a lumbering style, became a very effective bowler for England in the mid-2000s, and was a key man in the 2005 Ashes triumph. A taller man, Giles didn't worry so much about turn, bowling a flatter trajectory and concentrating on building pressure on the batsman mainly from a more defensive over-the-wicket line.

Vettori was the more naturally talented bowler, as more than 300 Test wickets suggests, but by understanding his own limitations for a period Giles became as important to his side. As in other disciplines, the advice to the young, slow left-armer is to focus on learning to spin the ball and develop variation, but if this is hard to come by then there are worse people to copy than Ashley Giles.

Daniel Vettori (left) and Ashley Giles (right) – two left-arm spinners with varying styles.

What it does

The left-arm spinner's stock delivery to a right-handed batsman will turn from leg-stump to off-stump. When bowled well, it will curve (gently swing) into the right-hander and then turn away towards the off-stump on landing.

How to do it

 The action is the mirror image to that of the off spinner (see page 81).

Murali Kartik on left-arm spin and advice for spinners

Should a left-arm spinner always look to come over the wicket to the right-handed batsman?

Generally left-arm spinners should look to come around the wicket to right-handed batsmen as it brings lots of decisions (LBW for example), in favour of the bowler. It's a more attacking option to get the batter out. Bowling over the wicket is a variation.

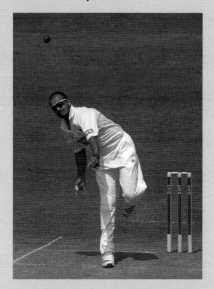

How important are turn and flight?

A bowler needs to spin the ball to be called a spinner, so it's very important. If you don't spin it, you are just a slow bowler. Flight plays a major part, too, in deceiving the batsmen and putting more character on the ball in terms of drift and bounce.

How should a spinner cope with the expectation of bowling on a turning pitch?

You don't have to try to do much. The key is to bowl the correct length depending on the height of the batsman and the wicket; this will do the job. On turning pitches it's easier for batsmen to hit big shots and harder to rotate the strike.

What advice would you give to the spinner?

Don't try to bowl a magic ball every ball.

Murali Kartik played eight Tests for India between 2000 and 2004

Over or around the wicket

Angles/subtlety for left-arm bowlers

The slow left-armer has a natural advantage over his right-arm counterpart as the ball, spinning away from the right-handed batsman, will cause more problems than the off-spinner.

Left-arm round the wicket use of crease

A slow left-armer might alternate between three delivery positions – mid-crease, wide on the crease or close to the stumps. This tactic is used to confuse the batsman and to deceive him, as different angle and spin of the delivery will be affected. This is also an effective tactic to use when the slow left-armer delivers his arm ball.

The left-armer can also influence the batsman's thinking by choosing whether or not to impart drift. By following through the action, with the bowling hand passing the right pocket, the ball will drift in. By allowing the bowling arm to complete past the left pocket will allow the ball to either hold its line or even drift away.

Left-arm over the wicket

Use of crease (varying the delivery position between mid-crease/wide/close to stumps) is again vital. In a four-day game there is normally a lot of rough for the slow left-armer to exploit, created by the footmarks of the right-arm over bowler. The turn of the ball should be exaggerated from this rough, and the same can be true if the bowler is bowling on a pitch that has been used previously. Bowling into these footmarks can be employed as a defensive tactic to the right-handed batsman, who will be wary at playing aggressively at a ball pitching in footmarks outside his leg-stump.

VARIATIONS
Arm ball

What it is

As for the off-break bowler, this is a ball that swings in the air.

What it does

This delivery will drift (swing) from the off-stump towards leg-stump.

How to do it

No spin is imported on the ball. Finger stays behind the ball on release, shiny side of the ball on the off-side. If the batsman leads his front leg to the line of the ball or looking to leave the ball outside the off-stump, the arm ball has every chance of either getting bowled or getting an LBW decision.

Bowler to study

DANIEL VETTORI (New Zealand 1997–)
Vettori runs the ball on to the right-hander from around the wicket with no evident change in the action and gets a lot of LBW decisions.

Top spinner

What it is

As for the off-break bowler, this is a ball that deceives batsmen in the flight.

What it does

The top-spinner has an upright seam. The delivery doesn't turn a great deal but dips earlier than the batsman anticipates and bounces higher/lower depending on the pitch conditions.

How to do it

 It is released from a higher position. The delivery is most effective when used against the sweep shot (extra bounce can lead to a top edge) and when the batsman is looking to come down the pitch, as the ball will dip earlier on him than he expects. If the pitch happens to be soft, then it may grip on the surface and stay low.

Left-arm unorthodox/Chinaman

What it is

The Chinaman bowler takes his name from Ellis Edgar Achong, a left-arm orthodox spinner of Chinese origin who played for the West Indies between 1929 and 1935, who could bowl a ball that turned the other way. Very few Chinaman bowlers have played Test cricket. The South African Paul Adams, Australia's Brad Hogg and Sir Garfield Sobers are examples. Adams is an example of a Chinaman bowler who adopted the googly as his stock delivery, turning the ball away from the right-handed batsman.

How to do it

 This delivery will spin from off-stump to leg-stump. It is bowled by a left-arm wrist-spinner normally from over the wicket.

Action

The action is mirrored to that of the right-arm leg-break bowler. The major difference is that the ball spins in a clockwise motion, which is opposite to the leg-spinner. The main dismissal method for a Chinaman bowler to a right-handed batsman would be LBW or bowled between bat and pad.

Variations

The googly, the top spinner and the flipper. Again, these deliveries are mirror images as for the leg-break bowler.

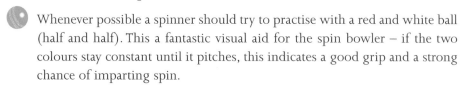

It is just as important for a spin bowler to be aggressive as it is a fast bowler. We play at a very high level of arousal, on the edge of fury if you like.

SHANE WARNE, APOLOGISING FOR HIS ABUSE OF SOUTH AFRICA'S ANDREW HUDSON IN JOHANNESBURG. WARNE WAS FINED AND WIDELY CONDEMNED DURING THE 1993/94 SEASON

Practice drills for all spinners

 Whenever possible a spinner should try to practise with a red and white ball (half and half). This a fantastic visual aid for the spin bowler – if the two colours stay constant until it pitches, this indicates a good grip and a strong chance of imparting spin.

 Work with a partner, 10 feet apart; throw a tennis ball to each other, bouncing once. Emphasise the index finger working down the ball to enable the ball to spin. Use a line in a sports hall or a piece of string for a visual aid and line.

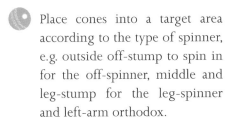 From the static position, move back and introduce a run-up, again using the line or rope as a visual guide.

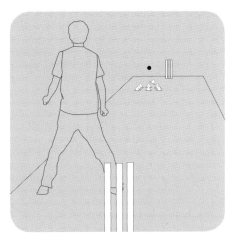

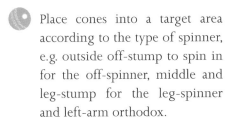 Place cones into a target area according to the type of spinner, e.g. outside off-stump to spin in for the off-spinner, middle and leg-stump for the leg-spinner and left-arm orthodox.

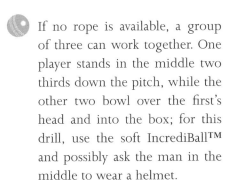 To encourage flight (getting the ball above the batsman's eyeline), tie a rope two-thirds of the way down the pitch just above head height. Then place cones in a box shape on a good length. The bowler has to get the ball up and over the rope but land it in the box and spin the ball. The ball must be delivered with energy.

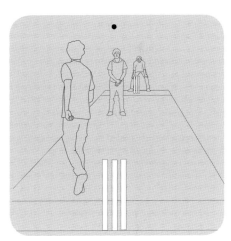

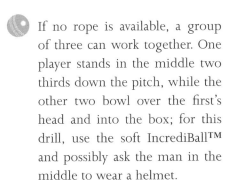 If no rope is available, a group of three can work together. One player stands in the middle two thirds down the pitch, while the other two bowl over the first's head and into the box; for this drill, use the soft IncrediBall™ and possibly ask the man in the middle to wear a helmet.

Quicker deliveries: with the rope still in place, try to bowl under the target; this should be a quicker and flatter delivery. Get a partner or coach to stand at the batsman's end. The bowler should now try both disciplines of bowling over and under the rope; asking the coach or partner to call out what they think they have bowled. The bowler is trying to deceive and confuse the batsman so vary the speed of approach to give him no obvious signs of what delivery is coming.

Problems and fixes for all spinners

- *The action isn't strong enough at the crease.* The bowler may be running in too fast – they should slow down and allow their action to flow.

- *Run-up too slow.* No momentum through the crease means the bowler will have to rely on their shoulders to compensate.

- *Dragging the ball down.* The front arm needs to be stronger.

- *Not spinning the ball (undercutting).* Check the grip, the position of the wrist on release and the alignment (feet/hips/shoulders).

- *Can't complete the action.* The delivery stride may be too big preventing the arms from following through fully.

- *Falling towards the off-side early in the delivery.* Keep the eyes level and focused on the target area, check the non-bowling arm is strong and driving down the wicket to the target area.

- *Getting hit out of the attack early.* The bowler shouldn't be frightened to start with fielders out to give confidence.

LIMITED-OVERS BOWLING

5.

INTRODUCTION

Bowling in one-day cricket can be a thankless task, certainly at international level where pitches are produced to aid run-scoring, and no-one is much interested in a game where bowlers dominate and they all have to go home early.

Things are a little different down the rungs, but the format is still geared towards the batsmen. Big hitting, lots of sixes – even more so in the Twenty20 game that has become so prominent in recent years.

But keep running in; there is a lot to keep the bowler interested in limited-overs cricket. Slower-balls, yorkers, subtle changes in line and length, there is a lot to be said for limited-overs cricket in terms of bowler development – all of these extra weapons are of use in the declaration game.

Wickets become marginally less important in the one-day game, with emphasis given to creating and sustaining pressure on the batsman. So it's good for accuracy and consistency too.

Basic principles of one-day bowling

- **Economy** becomes a key factor.
- It is important to take wickets but **pressure** created by restricting the runs scored will force the batting side to take risks.
- **Bowl to set plans** and field-placements to help create the pressure.
- **Bowl tighter lines**. Do not give the batsman width outside the off-stump, and anything down the leg-side is a wide.
- Depending on the surface, the bowler and the stage of the game, a bowler's stock delivery in one-day cricket might be moved to **back of a length** rather than a good length.
- **Variation of speed** can be as useful as lateral movement.
- If a bowling side can **win the initial power** play, and the death overs, they give themselves a good chance of winning the match.

- It is crucial to **start and finish the over well**, thus putting the pressure on the batsman rather than the bowler.
- In **Twenty20** cricket a bowler who goes for a **run-a-ball or under** is having a phenomenal game.
- In **50-over cricket** an economy rate of **under-four an over** is excellent.
- Seam bowlers should look to develop skills for **bowling at the death** (see below).

Bowling to an aggressive batsman

- If a batsman is playing aggressively at every ball the slower-ball variations will become very important.
- If they're a front-foot aggressive player then the short-of-a-length ball is best employed.
- Against someone who is very strong on the back-foot the bowler can look to use yorkers, or even the slower ball bouncer.
- If a batsman uses their feet to a pace bowler the bowler can try to bounce them. A medium-pacer might ask the keeper to come up to the stumps. The bowler could also use this tactic if a batsman is batting well out of their crease to try and disrupt the bowler's length.
- If the batsman is moving their feet, try to cramp them for room and follow their feet. But beware of the bluff.
- The bowler should think on their feet at all times, their game plans must be flexible to the situation and the batsman.
- The bowler should watch the batsman even when they aren't bowling at them. What are their scoring areas and shots? Do they hold the bat low down? Watch where they look. The bowler can give themselves a significant advantage.
- Move the field occasionally, just to keep the batsman thinking as to the bowler's intentions.
- The key thing is for the bowler not to allow the batsman to be set to a type of bowling. Changes of line, length and pace become more important.
- In nets or middle-practices, a bowler should try to bowl at the sloggers from time to time to try to work out where they will be trying to hit the ball so there is a scenario in place for a match situation.

Death bowling

- The bowler must be up for the challenge of bowling at the end of the innings, and must relish the opportunity to pick up wickets and be the hero for their team.
- When selecting their stock delivery to bowl at the end of the innings, the bowler must be flexible – they may have to change depending on the type of batsman they are facing. On some days they may not be able to hit the right areas so a back-up plan is essential.
- Variations to complement the stock delivery are vital. If the bowler has none then they will allow the batsman to get set against the same pace delivery and potentially take control of the innings.
- Variations (use of crease when bowling slower balls) to a good stock ball will keep the batsman guessing and the bowler one step ahead and in control.
- Watch the batsman. As the bowler walks back to their bowling marker they should turn and face the batsman and see where they are looking, this may give the bowler an idea of where the batsman is going to play. As the bowler is about to deliver, they should watch if the batsman moves around the crease; the batsman may look to go to one side in particular and this shows where their strengths are.
- The bowler must look to make sure they control the areas they get hit into e.g. full and straight deliveries with long-on and long-off in place. The bowler is then bowling to their field.
- Back of a length and bouncers. The bowler will be getting hit square of the wicket so this is where they must place your outfielders.
- Reverse swinging yorkers are a major weapon at the end of the innings.

Key points

- Be confident
- Be in control of emotions
- Be patient
- Thrive on the situation

Arul Suppiah on bowling spin in Twenty20 and limited-overs cricket

As a spinner how does your game-plan change when playing Twenty20?

In Twenty20 my game-plan is just to concede one run a ball, if I take a wicket that's a bonus. If I go for six an over that's good, dots balls are a bonus.

Do you give the ball more flight or less?

It all depends on the wicket and batsmen. Generally I try to bowl back of a length – a length where it's not easy to get underneath or not too short. I might give more air or flight if it's a turning wicket or a new batsman.

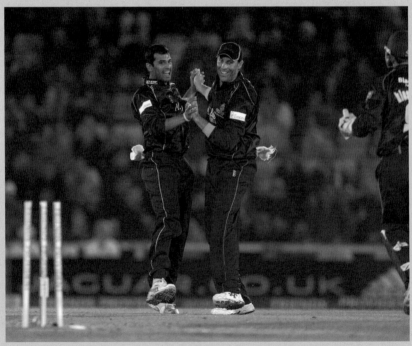

Arul Suppiah (left) celebrates a wicket with Somerset captain Marcus Trescothick.

Setting the field

There are a number of things the bowler should consider regarding field positions: the type of bowler, the pitch conditions, is the team defending or attacking, and the type of game. Remember the bowler needs to control the batsman. The bowler should be aware of what type of batsman they are bowling at and their strengths and weaknesses. A good bowler will force the batsman to play in areas they don't want or feel comfortable doing. The bowler's main objectives are to take wickets and stop runs being scored. By drying up the runs, pressure will build on the batting side. The bowler must be proactive. Something as simple as moving a fielder a couple of paces will provoke thoughts from the batsman as to where and why the bowler has made that change, sowing a seed of doubt in the batsman's mind. Cricket can be a game of chess and bluff.

Basic principles to follow
* Best fielders in key positions: specific to the game.
* Attack new batsmen.
* A bowler should take responsibility for their own field – too often the captain sets it without discussion with the bowler, the bowler must work closely with the captain.
* Attack whenever possible.
* Work out the batsman's strength/weakness.
* A bowler should look to make the batsman play in the areas they want them to, the bowler dictates where the ball goes.

THE MENTAL SIDE OF BOWLING

6.

KIT
Boots
All the bowler needs is a good pair of boots and his whites. It's worth a bowler investing in a decent pair of bowling boots, which differ from batting boots in that they have higher ankle supports. Investigate which boots are best when it comes to support, shock-absorption and comfort – it'll be worth it in the long run. Quick bowlers, certainly those aged 13 and over, should be looking to buy boots with full spikes, while spinners can get away with half-spikes. Spikes are important to help the bowler's feet grip during the run-up, delivery stride and follow-through. A bowler should be sure to wear in new boots gradually, otherwise they might get some painful blisters if they wear them straight away in a match.

Clothing
When it comes to clothing it's important that the bowler's muscles stay as warm and loose as possible, to help prevent injury. The bowler might consider wearing a T-shirt or vest under his shirt, even in warm conditions, as well as putting a sweater on after completing an over. It might feel too hot, but it's worth it.

PRE-MATCH PREPARATION FOR BOWLERS
Kit bag checking is of vital importance; ensure bowling boots are in good condition and clean. All studs should be tightened and spare studs available.

Try to have water bottles readily available in the bag along with fruit for energy.

A bowler will find that looking after their feet will prove a significant factor; they should ensure they have the correct socks with them – long and comfortable.

A thorough stretch during the warm-up is also vital. A routine within a warm-up should be followed when stretching before every match.

The bowler should have a look at the pitch before the toss; thinking about what lengths and lines they would look to bowl, taking into account possible areas to exploit. Inspect the landing area if it is a used pitch, along with the run-ups to see whether they're firm ground or soft. Also check to see any humps or bumps in the run-up areas or whether there is a slope. Have a look to see what direction the wind is blowing in as well.

Pre-match bowl-throughs are important too; try to do these as close to the pitch as possible, but be wary of not bowling on the square before the match has begun and conform to the regulations. A bowler should bowl from both ends during the warm-up to make sure they've had a feel for the conditions. The use of cones to practise line and length may be useful. During the bowling specific warm-up, the bowler should be sure to gather rhythm and momentum so they can take this straight onto the field with them during the match. It's worth the bowler informing the captain of the end they would prefer to bowl from, but be prepared to be flexible and for occasionally not bowling from the preferred end.

The bowler must consider their game plan for the type of pitch; field placements and the line and length to be bowled will be important. If the bowler has played against the opposition before, they should be aware of the batsman's strengths and weaknesses. If not, look for signs early in the game; for example, how the batsman sets up, how they grip the bat (low bottom hand on the bat may indicate the batsman is likely to cut and pull often). Another factor may be whether they look to get on the front foot often; this will help the bowler formulate a plan on how to contain the batsman, but essentially, get them out.

The bowler should focus on their own strengths; whether it's good line and length or if it's attacking with the new ball, the bowler should aim to use this strength to exploit the batsman's weaknesses. Prepare to be patient as the wicket or conditions may not create many early opportunities to take wickets. Be prepared to work hard and the bowler should always want the ball in their hand to bowl even if it's on a flat wicket.

POST-MATCH EVALUATION

The bowler should be honest with themselves on how they have performed. They should ask themselves if there was anything they could have done differently. Check the bowling figures against the scorebook and write down what went well and what didn't. They should evaluate what will need to improve before their next match or training session, but they should always remember to **look for positive aspects in their own performance.**

The bowler can use mental, physical and tactical wagon wheels to evaluate and improve their overall game. During the winter and summer, it is a good idea to check how development is going.

The creation of the wagon wheel can be checked over key stages during the year as it's a clear indication of strengths and weaknesses. The bowler will quickly see where improvements have been made and where their attention needs to focus. Create three wagon wheels and mark out of ten each heading. Colour the chart in, then aim to improve the weak areas, but don't forget to maintain the good ones.

FITNESS

Fitness and strength are important for the young cricketer. If a bowler is going to bowl a lot of overs and stand in the field all day they want to be sure they're in the best condition possible.

Every age cricketer has different fitness needs. We recommend a bowler speaks to their coach, or somebody at their local gym, to help them work out a fitness programme that suits them personally.

THE DREADED YIPS

People often say bowlers have it easier than batsmen, because a batsman only gets one chance while the bowler has six to take a wicket. That is true to a degree, but for the bowler who is having a bad day the extra exposure can be humiliating. A batsman can get off the pitch and sulk in the pavilion, while a bowler is forced to complete the over, and worse, possibly even bowl another one, then forced to field when he wants the ground to swallow him up.

The bowler who's having a really bad day might even be suffering a mild case of the yips, a mental affliction that arrives without warning and stops the bowler from being able to release the ball at the right time in their delivery stride. The yips have ruined the careers of several bowlers, mainly spinners but those are rare, extreme cases.

Changing your thought process

Is a bowler struggling with confidence? There are simple ways for them to change the way they go about their bowling.
- To be consistently successful they should believe that they are capable of meeting the challenges and demands set before them.
- They should know that the training that they have done is more than sufficient for them to succeed.
- They should maintain high levels of self-belief throughout.

To avoid negative thoughts and personal doubts of their ability, they should create a personal list of positive statements that specifically apply to them. Examples below.

- I can perform well under pressure
- I feel mentally tough
- I have trained well and am well prepared
- I am ready for tough situations
- I feel confident with my game
- I believe I can achieve anything

The bowler should repeat these regularly, selecting an up-to-date list and placing it in their cricket bag. They should read it on occasions when they may feel stressed or negative about their game.

Change from negative self-talk to positive self-talk
How to change self-talk
Negative opening
I can't ... I'm worried ... If only ... I hope ... It's difficult ...

Positive opening
I can if ... I'll be fine if ... When ... It is a challenge ...

Negative
I'm worried about bowling at that aggressive opening batsman.
That umpire has probably cost us the game.
I can't get that mistake out of my mind.

Positive
I'll be fine against the aggressive opening batsman as long as I stay calm.
We'll have to win this without any help from the umpire but we can still do it.
Give me another chance. I'll nail it next time.

PRACTICE, PRACTICE, PRACTICE

INTRODUCTION

A bowler can read this book as many times as they like, but if they don't put in the hours alone or in the nets practising the skills they've read about, they'll never be the bowler they can be.

Practice should never be a drag. A bowler should work hard on their faults, be self-aware but never overly self-critical.

The bowler has got to put the work in, but shouldn't over-practise. Practising the same skill for a prolonged period of time might exhaust certain muscles. If a bowler is practising when tired then they may be teaching themselves bad habits. A bowler should listen to their body.

PLANNING YOUR WINTER AND SUMMER

If a player doesn't have access to a local school or county coach, then it's worth them going down to their local club to see if there's someone who can help. It is important to formulate a plan for winter development. This should begin with a chat about how the player's summer performances went. From this the player can work out what areas they need to develop during the winter.

All cricketers should keep a diary and write up their interpretation of coaching sessions, diet and fitness routine. During the cricket season they should record runs scored, wickets taken and how they got out, or which type of bowler took their wicket each time. From this the player may find a common denominator to work on in their winter training programme.

Each month a review with the coach is advisable – has the player mastered what they set out to do? What do they want to work on next, e.g. away swing, slower balls? These things can take a long time to address. Fitness and fielding are equally important. In the modern game a player should look to become a specialist in the field as well as in their other chosen discipline.

Net practice

When the winter technical work is well under way, it is useful to have the occasional net session to see if the initial changes are successful. Early winter nets serve little or no purpose if a player is making changes to their game. Nets merely reinforce a player's faults.

- The bowler should step away or work solely on their skills by bowling at cones and targets in the nets. **Two months before the start of the season** is the time to start netting regularly against batsmen to monitor how successful any changes have become (possibly use a video camera).
- Once the bowler is comfortable with the above it is then appropriate to introduce scenarios to their net sessions. They should discuss with the batsman a match situation. Set the field and after three overs discuss how it went. They may want to work on their slower deliveries, or bowling at the death. Whatever it is, they should engage with it and try and make the situation as realistic as possible.

THE FUTURE

Cricketers who aspire to either go and play professional cricket or reach their highest possible level are increasingly becoming aware of the needs of the modern player. Professional counties demand two or three-dimensional players – fitness and fielding are as important as batting and bowling, while diet and nutrition are now key components for every player.

All cricketers with ambitions of playing regularly should join their local cricket team if they haven't already done so. If you are a younger player you should look for a thriving youth section and active coaches within the club. Are young players being integrated into the senior sides? Is it a multi-sports facility where perhaps the whole family can join and enjoy all the facilities? Encourage your friends to attend. You could then get a group to practise together during the evenings and school holidays.

An older player should look for a club with a good net culture, and teams for a range of abilities.

ADVICE FOR COACHES

There are two types of coaches, a tell coach and a delivery coach.

The discovery coach allows the batsman to explore options. Each player is unique and individual and, although the basic techniques should be adhered to, it's great for inexperienced players to show flare, initiative to excite, to challenge and to discuss.

A coach can hope to give his players a complete understanding of their game, be it technical, tactical, physical or mental and to realise their full potential. Whether you play at international, county, club or social level, enjoyment is the priority and your game will certainly be enhanced if you enjoy it.

Coaching sessions should be relaxed – a coach should try to make sure that the players believe that they are most important. A coach has to earn their trust and respect for it is then that the relationship between coach and student can really flourish. Encouragement is important but it's also a good idea to constantly challenge pupils to get out of their comfort zone for them to improve their game.

A really enjoyable aspect of coaching is problem-solving. Some coaches look for things that simply aren't there just to justify their existence, but it is equally important on occasions to say nothing except 'well played'. It can give a coach huge satisfaction when major/minor changes can make such a difference and improve the individual game.

Some boys and players struggle when moving school or club – they get big fish/small pond syndrome so they may drift away from the game due to fear of failure and not being centre of attention like they were in their previous school or club. The key to success is to embrace all challenges, have an open mind and be able to discuss things with someone.

Player and coach relationship
What the coach should remember

- Allow the pupil to become independent but be able to discuss things openly.
- Coaching is not about the pupil hanging on the coach's every word.
- Don't over coach. You are educating the player to think for themselves while maintaining a close working relationship with the coach.
- You should be encouraging the player to explore all avenues of their game, and find out what works for them.

What the player should remember

- Enjoy the game.
- The coach is there to help you fulfil your potential and stretch you to the limits.
- Treat the coach with the respect with which you would like to be treated.

APPENDIX

MODES OF DISMISSAL

1. **Caught:** When the ball is caught on the full by a member of the fielding side after it has touched the batsman's bat, or the batsman's glove while their hand is on the bat.

2. **Bowled:** When the ball is bowled to the striking batsman and dislodges the bails from the stumps at the striker's end.

3. **Leg before wicket (LBW):** The LBW rule is complex, so we've included the whole law.

    The striker is out LBW in the circumstances set out below.

    (a) The bowler delivers a ball, not being a no ball and

    (b) the ball, if it is not intercepted full pitch, pitches in line between wicket and wicket or on the off-side of the striker's wicket and

    (c) the ball not having previously touched their bat, the striker intercepts the ball, either full pitch or after pitching, with any part of their person and

    (d) the point of impact, even if above the level of the bails, either (i) is between wicket and wicket or (ii) if the striker has made no genuine attempt to play the ball with their bat, is either between wicket and wicket or outside the line of the off stump and

    (e) but for the interception, the ball would have hit the wicket.

4. **Run out:** When a fielder, bowler or wicket-keeper removes one or both of the bails with the ball by hitting the stumps when a batsman is out of their ground attempting a run. If the bails have been removed, then the fielding side can remove a stump from the ground and as long as it is in contact with the ball the batsman is still run out.

5. **Stumped:** When the wicket-keeper removes the bails while the striking batsman is out of his crease. This sort of dismissal will occur when the wicket-keeper is standing up to the stumps.

6. **Hit wicket:** When the striking batsman dislodges the bails during or in the immediate aftermath of a delivery.

7. **Handled the ball:** When the batsman deliberately handles the ball without the permission of the fielding team.

8. Hit the ball twice: When the batsman deliberately strikes the ball a second time, except for the sole purpose of guarding his wicket.

9. Obstructing the field: When a batsman deliberately stops a fielder from attempting to field the ball, or throw at the stumps.

10. Timed out: When a new batsman takes more than three minutes to take their position in the field to replace a dismissed batsman. (If the delay is protracted, the umpires may cause the match to be forfeited.)

Miscellany

A batsman can leave the field without being dismissed if they are injured or ill. The batsman is not out; they may return to bat later in the same innings if sufficiently recovered. Also, an unimpaired batsman may retire, in which case they are treated as being dismissed retired out.

An individual cannot be out — bowled, caught, leg before wicket, stumped, or hit wicket off a no ball.

The batsman who is not on strike may be run out by the bowler if they leave their crease before the bowler bowls, and a batsman can be out obstructing the field or retired out at any time. Timed out by its nature is a dismissal without a delivery. With all other modes of dismissal, only one batsman can be dismissed per ball bowled. Obstructing the field, handled the ball, timed out and hit the ball twice dismissals are extremely rare.

MISCELLANEOUS

The following taken from the MCC's *Laws of Cricket*. Please refer to the laws in full for a complete explanation.

The no-ball rule

1. **Mode of delivery**

   (a) The umpire shall ascertain whether the bowler intends to bowl right handed or left handed, over or round the wicket, and shall so inform the striker. It is unfair if the bowler fails to notify the umpire of a change in his mode of delivery. In this case the umpire shall call and signal No ball.

   (b) Underarm bowling shall not be permitted except by special agreement before the match.

2. **Fair delivery – the arm**

   For a delivery to be fair in respect of the arm the ball must not be thrown. See 3 below. Although it is the primary responsibility of the striker's end umpire to assess the fairness of a delivery in this respect, there is nothing in this Law to debar the bowler's end umpire from calling and signalling No ball if he considers that the ball has been thrown.

(a) If, in the opinion of either umpire, the ball has been thrown, he shall call and signal No ball and, when the ball is dead, inform the other umpire of the reason for the call. The bowler's end umpire shall then

    (i)   caution the bowler. This caution shall apply throughout the innings.

    (ii)   inform the captain of the fielding side of the reason for this action.

    (iii) inform the batsmen at the wicket of what has occurred.

(b) If, after such caution, either umpire considers that, in that innings, a further delivery by the same bowler is thrown, the procedure set out in (a) above shall be repeated, indicating to the bowler that this is a final warning. This warning shall also apply throughout the innings.

(c) If either umpire considers that, in that innings, a further delivery by the same bowler is thrown, he shall call and signal No ball and when the ball is dead inform the other umpire of the reason for the call. The bowler's end umpire shall then

    (i)   direct the captain of the fielding side to suspend the bowler forthwith. The over shall, if applicable, be completed by another bowler, who shall neither have bowled the previous over or part thereof nor be allowed to bowl any part of the next over. The bowler thus suspended shall not bowl again in that innings.

    (ii)   inform the batsmen at the wicket and, as soon as practicable, the captain of the batting side of the occurrence.

(d) The umpires together shall report the occurrence as soon as possible after the match to the Executive of the fielding side and to any Governing Body responsible for the match, who shall take such action as is considered appropriate against the captain and the bowler concerned.

3. **Definition of fair delivery – the arm**

A ball is fairly delivered in respect of the arm if, once the bowler's arm has reached the level of the shoulder in the delivery swing, the elbow joint is not straightened partially or completely from that point until the ball has left the hand. This definition shall not debar a bowler from flexing or rotating the wrist in the delivery swing.

4. **Bowler throwing towards striker's end before delivery**

If the bowler throws the ball towards the striker's end before entering his delivery stride, either umpire shall call and signal No ball. See Law 42.16 (Batsmen stealing a run). However, the procedure stated in 2 above of caution, informing, final warning, action against the bowler and reporting shall not apply.

5. **Fair delivery – the feet**

For a delivery to be fair in respect of the feet, in the delivery stride

(a) the bowler's back foot must land within and not touching the return crease appertaining to his stated mode of delivery.

(b) the bowler's front foot must land with some part of the foot, whether grounded or raised

(i)   on the same side of the imaginary line joining the two middle stumps as the return crease described in (a) above and

(ii) behind the popping crease.

If the bowler's end umpire is not satisfied that all of these three conditions have been met, he shall call and signal No ball.

6. **Ball bouncing more than twice or rolling along the ground**

The umpire shall call and signal No ball if a ball which he considers to have been delivered, without having previously touched bat or person of the striker, either

(i)   bounces more than twice or

(ii) rolls along the ground before it reaches the popping crease.

7. **Ball coming to rest in front of striker's wicket**

If a ball delivered by the bowler comes to rest in front of the line of the striker's wicket, without having previously touched the bat or person of the striker, the umpire shall call and signal No ball and immediately call and signal Dead ball.

8. **Call of No ball for infringement of other Laws**

In addition to the instances above, No ball is to be called and signalled as required by the following Laws.

Law 40.3 – Position of wicket-keeper

Law 41.5 – Limitation of on side fielders

Law 41.6 – Fielders not to encroach on pitch

Law 42.6 – Dangerous and unfair bowling

Law 42.7 – Dangerous and unfair bowling - action by the umpire

Law 42.8 – Deliberate bowling of high full pitched balls

9. **Revoking a call of No ball**

An umpire shall revoke his call of No ball if the ball does not leave the bowler's hand for any reason.

10. **No ball to over-ride Wide**

A call of No ball shall over-ride the call of Wide ball at any time. See Laws 25.1 (Judging a Wide) and 25.3 (Call and signal of Wide ball).

11. **Ball not dead**

The ball does not become dead on the call of No ball.

12. **Penalty for a No ball**

A penalty of one run shall be awarded instantly on the call of No ball. Unless the call is revoked, the penalty shall stand even if a batsman is dismissed. It shall be in addition to any other runs scored, any boundary allowance and any other runs awarded for penalties.

13. **Runs resulting from a No ball – how scored**

The one run penalty shall be scored as a No ball extra. If other penalty runs have been awarded to either side these shall be scored as stated in Law 42.17 (Penalty runs). Any runs completed by the batsmen or any boundary allowance shall be credited to the striker if the ball has been struck by the bat; otherwise they shall also be scored as No ball extras. Apart from any award of 5 penalty runs, all runs resulting from a No ball, whether as No ball extras or credited to the striker, shall be debited against the bowler.

14. **No ball not to count**

A No ball shall not count as one of the over. See Law 22.3 (Validity of balls).

15. **Out from a No ball**

When No ball has been called, neither batsman shall be out under any of the Laws except 33 (Handled the ball), 34 (Hit the ball twice), 37 (Obstructing the field) or 38 (Run out).

© *Marylebone Cricket Club 2010*

The wide rule

1. **Judging a Wide**

   (a) If the bowler bowls a ball, not being a No ball, the umpire shall adjudge it a Wide if, according to the definition in (b) below, in his opinion the ball passes wide of the striker where he is and which also would have passed wide of him standing in a normal guard position.

   (b) The ball will be considered as passing wide of the striker unless it is sufficiently within his reach for him to be able to hit it with his bat by means of a normal cricket stroke.

2. **Delivery not a Wide**

   The umpire shall not adjudge a delivery as being a Wide

   (a) if the striker, by moving, either

       (i)   causes the ball to pass wide of him, as defined in 1(b) above or

(ii) brings the ball sufficiently within his reach to be able to hit it by means of a normal cricket stroke.

(b) if the ball touches the striker's bat or person.

3. **Call and signal of Wide ball**

(a) If the umpire adjudges a delivery to be a Wide he shall call and signal Wide ball as soon as the ball passes the striker's wicket. It shall, however, be considered to have been a Wide from the instant of delivery, even though it cannot be called Wide until it passes the striker's wicket.

(b) The umpire shall revoke the call of Wide ball if there is then any contact between the ball and the striker's bat or person.

(c) The umpire shall revoke the call of Wide ball if a delivery is called a No ball. See Law 24.10 (No ball to over-ride Wide).

4. **Ball not dead**

The ball does not become dead on the call of Wide ball.

5. **Penalty for a Wide**

A penalty of one run shall be awarded instantly on the call of Wide ball. Unless the call is revoked (see 3(b) and (c) above), this penalty shall stand even if a batsman is dismissed, and shall be in addition to any other runs scored, any boundary allowance and any other runs awarded for penalties.

6. **Runs resulting from a Wide – how scored**

All runs completed by the batsmen or a boundary allowance, together with the penalty for the Wide, shall be scored as Wide balls. Apart from any award of 5 penalty runs, all runs resulting from a Wide shall be debited against the bowler.

7. **Wide not to count**

A Wide shall not count as one of the over. See Law 22.3 (Validity of balls).

8. **Out from a Wide**

When Wide ball has been called, neither batsman shall be out under any of the Laws except 33 (Handled the ball), 35 (Hit wicket), 37 (Obstructing the field), 38 (Run out) or 39 (Stumped).

ABOUT THE AUTHORS

ABOUT MARK DAVIS

Mark Davis was born in Kilve, West Somerset in 1962. A left-arm swing bowler, Mark played for Somerset between 1980 and 1987. During that time he opened the bowling with Ian Botham and Joel Garner. Other notable colleagues included Viv Richards, Martin Crowe and Vic Marks. Mark toured Zimbabwe with England 'A' in 1982, and after leaving the pro game he became a player-coach with Llangennech in the South Wales league, operating as a freelance coach in schools around Wiltshire, Dorset and Somerset. He joined Millfield as head coach in 1996, and has overseen the development of countless county players and a few international players since, as well as helping out at the Somerset academy. He has worked as an analyst on BBC Radio Bristol's cricket coverage since the early 1990s.

ABOUT SAM COLLINS

Sam Collins is a freelance cricket journalist and former editor of thewisdencricketer.com, who has previously worked for CricInfo and Guardian. co.uk.

Away from journalism Sam is a former Kent Under-19 opening bowler and captained Eton College in 2001. He still plays cricket when time allows.

AUTHORS' NOTE

All the explanations in this book are for a right-arm over the wicket bowler unless otherwise stated.

ACKNOWLEDGEMENTS

The authors would like to thank their partners Sophie and Kim for all their patience and help; Chris Greenwood, Andrew Roberts and Joseph Dale for translating Mark's scribbles; Christopher Gange and Jarrod Kimber for their assistance with photography; and Millfield School pupils for their participation and enthusiasm in all photo shoots. Many thanks to others; there are just too many to mention: this would not have been possible without your help.